GREEK MYTHOLOGY

TO MY OWN
APHRODITE

CONTENTS

Greece was – and perhaps still is – above all, the land of myths.

A cultivated society, a language perfected through time, a people of insatiable curiousity, with an irresistible urge to explore, created a multiplicity of intricate, beautiful myths which, through the ages, have continued to inspire art and literature around the world.

At the dawn of civilization, ancient peoples, in their effort to interpret natural phenomena, comprehend abstract meaning or feelings while seeing the need for rules, moral guidance and natural order, attributed whatever they met with in their daily lives to higher powers.

The imaginative Greeks could not be satisfied by simple, primitive interpretations, but instead created a host of gods and divine beings and wove so many striking, strange and wonderful myths that today it is justly considered to be the richest and most interesting of all mythologies.

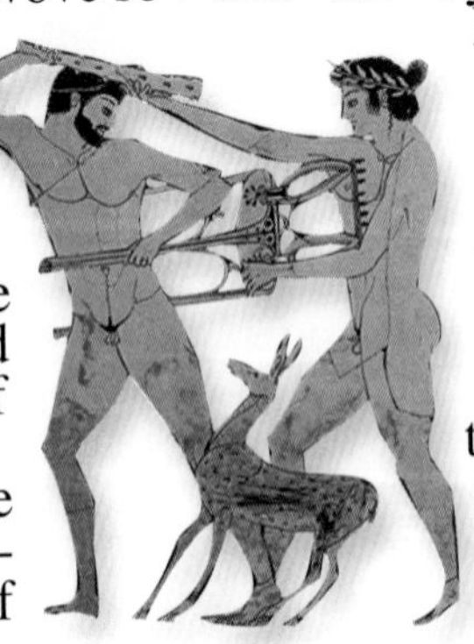

In contrast to the distant, often repulsive gods of other ancient peoples, the Greek gods seemed approachable, possessed with supernatural powers but human both in form and nature: imperfect, neither merciful nor just, swept by passions, revengeful, biased, lusting after each other and mortals, intervening in battle, taking the part of their chosen ones, demanding sacrifice, punishment or praise. Always the lines of contact with man are open, involving the gods in earthly and earthy intrigues.

And then there were the darker powers, often, like Pan, the satyrs or the centaurs, half animal, or demonic like the hundred-handed ones, the gorgons and the Cyclops which, however, were never deified.

Wanting to feel as close as they could to the nature and light of their country the Greeks deified and personified not just earthly and heavenly elements: sun, moon, rivers, but abstract ideas, such as divine justice (Nemesis), remorse (the Furies), justice (Thetis), love (Eros), death (Chairon) and the underworld with its own dark god.

As is the case with all primaeval myths, taboos are broken: there is copulation among siblings, mother and son, father and daughter, patricide, matricide, paedicide, going as far as fathers devouring their children, elements derived from earlier, more primitive states.

Drawing from inexhaustible wells of fantasy the Greeks enriched the mythological canvas with stories of their heroes and legends of the founding of cities and colonies, though, naturally, many of these myths lack chronologically consistency, owing both to the existence of many variations and the fact that they are, after all, myths, not history.

The Greek myths were sung* by ancient poets, first of all by Homer, followed by lyric poets and then gave inspiration to great dramatists who enriched them with every aspect of human nature: all the extremes of joy and suffering, reward and punishment, as well as teaching a moral in such a way that today their works are considered to be classical.

Thousands of Greek sculptures and bas-reliefs – including those of the Parthenon – vases and wall-paintings, illustrate the lives and deeds of mythical beings with a wealth of detail.

After the Renaissance, which based European culture on the study of the Ancient Greece, a host of dramatists wrote masterpieces based on Greek myths, great painters illustrated them, composers wrote operas, philosophers drew on them. Freud based a whole psychological theory on the Oedipus

**Literally, the poems would have been not just recited but sung by these early poets.*

myth, even the name of Europe derived from a beautiful erotic myth.

The word "mythology" itself, which has been absorbed into many languages, derives from two Greek words: "mythos" and "logos" ("story").

Naturally enough there came the time when the Greeks, with the development of logic and philosophy, would question the mythical accounts of the Creation and seek more firmly-based explanations, first of all from the pre-Socratic philosophers, for the origin of natural elements (air – water – earth). But the robust Greek myths were not so easily discarded and continued to be taught to the young, while even Herodotos, the "father of history" draws on many of them in his works.

The present volume is not intended for specialists or researchers into Greek myth, but aims to present, simply and clearly the most commonly accepted versions of the main myths, to familiarize the reader with the acts of gods and men and to draw from this inexhaustible educational source in order to raise awareness, please the spirit and instruct the soul. So let's open ourselves to the beauty, joy and inexhaustible richness of Greek mythology.

THE HISTORICITY OF THE MYTHS – SOURCES

Myths are often based on events that are subsequently found to be historically proven: with the excavations in the area of Ilium and the discovery of the burnt remains of Troy 1X, by **Heinrich Schliemann**, the Trojan War was dated somewhere in the 13th century B.C. **Mycenae**, also excavated by Schliemann, was shown to have reached its flowering ("golden Mycenae") at the same time. Sir Arthur Evans excavations at **Knossos** in Crete brought to light a labyrinthine palace whose wall-paintings bore out much that is mentioned in related myths.

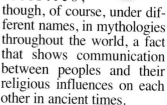

There are also certain important events that are registered in man's collective memory, such as The **Great Flood** which, in very similar form, enters into the mythology of the Greeks, Indians, Sumerians, Mayans and the Old Testament of the Jews. A similar case is the drowning of the mythical land of **Atlantis**. Generally many creation myths show similarities (e.g. the Kumarbi Epic of the Hittites and the Greek **Hesiod** with regard to the birth of Cronos) and, in addition, many gods have similar attributes and characteristics, though, of course, under different names, in mythologies throughout the world, a fact that shows communication between peoples and their religious influences on each other in ancient times.

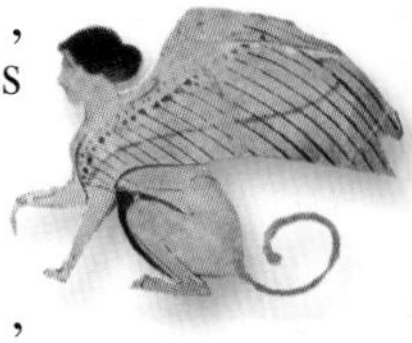

Our sources for all these Greek myths and their variants – who knows how many others, went unrecorded, or if recorded, have been lost? – are chiefly Hesiod (8th C. B.C.) who, in his works **Theogony** (the genesis of the gods and the dominion of the twelve Olympian deities) and **Work and Days** which deals with the creation of man; **Homer**, in his great epics, The **Iliad** and The **Odyssey** which were originally sung in the form of "rhapsodies" at the court of

Left: Detail from "The Abduction of Europe" by Nicolas Coypel (1690 – 1734).
Bottom: "The Apotheosis of Homer" by Jean Ingres (1780 – 1867).

chieftains, but by the 6th century B.C. had been written down and prescribed for the education of the young. Alexander the Great, for instance, always kept a copy of the Iliad under his pillow; **Orphic poems**, some of which are the most ancient to have come down to us, also give us a lot of information, es-pecially about the creation of the world and the gods. **Hecataeus** of **Milos** contributed greatly with his *Geneology* and "*Journey on Earth*", which included the first map of the then-known world; **Apollodoros** (2nd C. B.C.) in his *Library*; **Diodoros** of **Sicily**, (1st C. B.C.), as well as geographers, such as **Strabo** and travelers such as **Pausanius** who included in their works a wealth of local myths and legends which proved to be extraordinarily useful in the study of antiquity.

One of the basic factors, the knowledge of which helps us understand the space-time dimension of Greek myths, is the fact that ancient Greece was composed of numerous city-states, each with its own king, mythical hero, laws and customs and with interwoven histories, so that while we can see a hero taking part in a particular episode in a particular time and place, he may reappear - and not just once - in another time or place, generations apart.

Already in Ancient times Homer was held in the highest estimation, even being raised to a god-like status, this apotheosis being represented in fine sculptures and, later, in the works of famous painters.

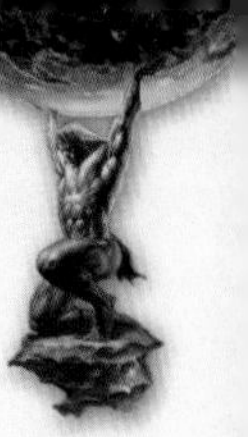

CREATION MYTHS

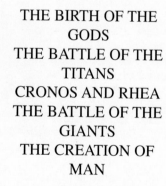

THE BIRTH OF THE GODS
THE BATTLE OF THE TITANS
CRONOS AND RHEA
THE BATTLE OF THE GIANTS
THE CREATION OF MAN

THE BIRTH OF THE GODS

Hesiod (8th C. B.C.), on whose works all we have to say about the Creation is based, gives us the most ancient and the most widely accepted account of the birth of the gods.

In the beginning, then, there were three divine, self-created elements: **Chaos**, **Gaia** (The Earth) and **Eros**. Of these three powers only Love was without issue, his role being to unite other life-giving forces, to be the "cause of everything" and to urge creation. He had no relation to the winged son of Aphrodite.

Without intercourse, Chaos gave birth to **Night** and **Erebos** (darkness) who in turn gave birth to **Aithera** (the air) and **Imera** (the day). Night, alone, gave birth to **Sleep**, **Death**, **Nemesis** (Divine Justice), **Deceit** and **Erida** (which breeds strife). Gaia, alone, gave birth to Uranos (the sky) , joining with him to form the first divine pair endowed with power and giving birth to the twelve **Titans**: Oceanos, Hyperion, Iapetos, Rhea, Themis, Mnimosini, Theia, Phoebe, Tithis, Koios, Crius and Cronos), the three **Cyclops** (gigantic beings who shared one eye), and three gigantic **Hundred-handed ones**. The Earth (Gaia) produced, by herself, **Pontos** (the deep sea), **Ori** (the mountains) and, in general, many natural features. Among her descendants were the three thousand daughters of Oceanos (The **Oceanides**, lake divinities), and his three thousand sons, the **Potamoi** (rivers) and, in addition, fifty beautiful water-nymphs, the **Nereids**, daughters of the aged Nirea (sea divinities) as well as the three **Harpies**, destructive divinities of wind and storm. Many of these divinities will be encountered or referred to in the following pages.

Top: Bust attributed to be that of Hesiod.
Centre: The Goddess Ivi. Detail of a painting by William Adolphe Bouguereau 1825 – 1905.
Bottom: Bronze Head of the God of Sleep. Roman copy, 1st C. A.D. British Museum, London.

Left: Roman copy of a statue of the Goddess Gaia.
Centre: Roman Mosaic of the God Pontus.
Bottom: The castration of Uranus by Cronus. Painting by Giorgio Vasari (1511 – 1574. Palazio Vecchio, Florence).

CRONOS & RHEA

Because **Uranos** feared that he might be usurped by one or more of the **Titans**, he imprisoned them in the bowels of Gaia, the Earth, who began to resent not just the weight on her but his behaviour towards her other children, and begged her youngest son, Cronos, to avenge her. Armed with a scythe, provided by his mother, Cronos waylaid Uranos and, after castrating him, threw the organs into the sea. From the sperm-foam arose the beautiful goddess **Aphrodite** (the first of the Olympian gods who afterwards came to power), while from the blood droplets that fell to earth were born the **Erynies** (guilt), the **Giants** and the **Meliae**, (or ash-nymphs).

Cronos seized power, freed his siblings and decreed that both Oceanos and Tethis would govern the seas, Hyperion and

Phoebe the sun and stars. After marrying his sister, Rhea, he started to have children. But since Uranus had prophesized that one of them would usurp Cronos's power, he forced his wife, each time she gave birth, to deliver the baby to him, which he swallowed. So he disposed of **Dimitra**, **Hestia**, **Poseidon**, **Hera**, and **Pluto**. Rhea, of course, could not stand this for long and, when Zeus was born, deceived Cronos, substituting a stone wrapped in swaddling clothes for the infant, and had the child sequestered in a cave (the Idaion Andron) on Mount Ida in Crete, where he was brought up by nymphs while the **Kourites** clashed their shields to smother the baby's cries and the goat **Amalthia** provided him with milk.

When Zeus came of age and was strong enough to stand up to Cronos, he forced him to swallow a herb which made him vomit up his children, after which Zeus, in his turn, seized power.

After he had married his sister, Hera, he shared lordship of the cosmos with his two brothers: to **Poseidon** he gave the governance of the sea, to **Pluto** the kingdom of the underworld, while he himself held sway over the sky and, of course, held precedence over all the other gods. Gradually, together with his sisters **Dimitra** and **Hestia**, with the help of **Aphrodite** and his own children: **Apollo**, **Artemis**, **Dionyssos**, **Athina**, **Ares**, **Hephaistos** and **Hermes**, he formed the group that

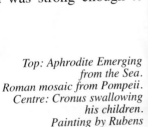

Top: Aphrodite Emerging from the Sea. Roman mosaic from Pompeii. Centre: Cronus swallowing his children. Painting by Rubens Bottom: Athenian pelike, 5th C. B.C. Rhea deceiving Cronos

Right: The infant Zeus being fed with the milk of Amaltheia. Jacob Jordaens - 1640)
Centre: Head of Rhea. 2nd C. B.C.
Bottom: The Battle of the Titans. Rubens.

would govern the universe, named, from the mountain from which all but Pluto ruled, the **Olympian Gods**. So they are portrayed on the east frieze of the Parthenon, presiding over the Panathinaion procession, in honour of the goddess Athina. (the New Acropolis Museum).

THE BATTLE OF THE TITANS

Before he had firmly established his power, Zeus had to face many problems created by the divinities who opposed him. His brothers, the **Titans**, refusing to accept the overlordship of a younger god, started a war that would involve all of the immortals.

The Titans, led by Cronos, barricaded themselves on Mount **Orthris**, while the followers of Zeus fortified neighbouring **Olympos**. The Titans, however, were not entirely united: on Zeus's side were the powerful Titaness **Stynx**, together with her children: Kratos (state), Via (violence), Zilos (jealousy) and Niki (victory), **Oceanos** and **Prometheus**

Right: Zeus combating the giant Porphyrion. (Attic kylix, 400 B.C.)

(son of the Titaness Iapetos), his chief adviser, together with his mother, the Titaness **Rhea**, **Themis**, **Mnimosini** (memory), **Phoebe** and **Tithos**. But the most decisive of all was his grandmother, **Gaia**, the Earth.

The terrible strife raged for ten years, shaking Creation to its foundations, but still the outcome was uncertain. It was then that Gaia chose to tell Zeus that, according to a prophecy, he would only be victorious if he released the **Cyclops** and the **Hundred-handed ones** from **Tartarus**. This Zeus accomplished, plunging deep into the bowels of the Earth, and the monsters he liberated joined with him and the Olympians, the Cyclops granting him the gift of thunder and lightning, Poseidon the Trident and Pluto the "kinea", a hood of dogskin which rendered the wearer invisible.

Armed thus the Olympians launched the final battle, the earth shaking and thundering, ending in their total victory. Zeus bestowed privileges on his brothers and sisters and hurled Cronos and his cohorts down into Tarturus, to be guarded by the Hundred-handed ones.

THE BATTLE OF THE GIANTS

The basic reason for the battle was both Gaia's dissatisfaction with the harsh punishment given to the Titans and with the increasing aloofness of the Olympians after the battle, who failed to afford her the necessary respect. Thus she decided to aid her youngest offspring, the **Giants**, to

Right: The tortures of Atlantas and Prometheus. Laconian amphora, 6th C. B.C. Vatican Museum.

Amongst all Zeus's opponents, the one who was punished most harshly was ***Atlas****, who was condemned for all eternity to bear the dome of the heavens on his shoulders (see Heracles, the Apple of the Hesperides). Atlas had seven beautiful daughters, the* ***Pleiades****, who unable to bear the sight of their suffering father, wee taken up into the skies and metamorphosed into the* ***galaxy of the Pleiades****.*

According to another myth, Atlas was the firstborn son of Poseidon who appointed him king of ***Atlantis****, beyond the oceans, the mythical lost island or continent known throughout the world.*

win power. The Giants, who had sprung from the blood of the castrated Uranus, were massive, monstrous beings with lizard-like tails and hair of snakes. They were, however, not immortal.

So the war started and Earth became hell again as the Giants launched a terrible battery of flaming trees and huge rocks, the sea boiled, mountains shifted, islands were drowned and rivers changed their flow. The Olympians resisted the attack with all their strength: Poseidon raised a whole island, Nisiros, and hurled it down onto the giant Polyvotis, crushing him. Athina, who had sprung from the head of Zeus during the battle, wiped out Pallanta, utilizing his skin to make the shield that rendered her invulnverable. She also

Above: The Pleiades metamorphosing into a galaxy. Painting by Ellihu Vedder. Metropolitan Museuam, New York.
Bottom: Scene from the Battle of the Giants.

hunted down Encelados and hurled Sicily onto him, the eruptions of whose volcano, Etna, were said to be his death-struggles. The struggle lasted many years and the geological disturbances seemingly unending until Zeus received a prophecy which told him that only if a mortal could be found to fight on his side could he be the victor. So he enlisted the aid of **Hercules**, Dia's favourite son.

With him on their side the Olympians managed gradually to wipe out the Giants. Gaia desperately tried to help them by providing them with a herb that would render them invincible, but Zeus, anticipating this, managed to steal the herb from her. So Zeus and his allies were victorious, established their rule over the earth and rebuilt their heavenly palace on Olympus, which had been damaged in the war.

Representations of the Battle of the Giants are to be found on many ceramics and sculptures, the most important being the Metopes from the east wing of the Parthenon (New Acropolis Museum) and the Pergamon altar (Berlin).

TYPHON

However, the annihilation of the Giants enraged Gaia so much that she paired with Tartarus and gave birth to **Typhon** (Typhoea),

Top: Poseidon confronting the giant Polybotis, watched by Gaia. Athenian calyx, 5th C. B.C. Archaeological Museum, Berlin.

Bottom: The Battle of the Giants. Painting by Perin del Vargas, 1533.

Top right: The fall of the Giants. Giulio Romano. 1499 – 1546.
Centre: Hercules aiming at the giant Porphyrion as he attacks Hera. Athenian amphora. 4th C. B.C. Louvre, Paris.
Bottom: Zeus hurling thunderbolts at Typhon..Hydria 6th C. B.C. Munich.

a monster of unconquerable strength, half human, half dragon, horribly disgusting in appearance.

When the Gods beheld this monster they metamorphosed into animals and fled to Egypt to hide them-

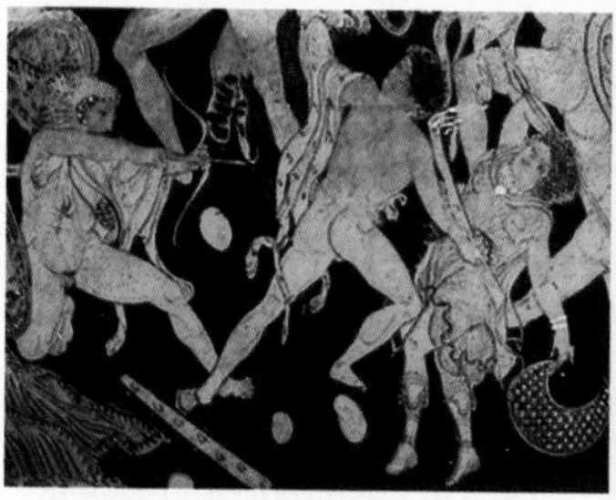

selves, only Zeus and his favourite daughter, Athena, remaining to stand against the monster.

The struggle between Zeus and Typhon was shattering. At one particular moment Typhon managed to enfold Zeus in his coils, cut and remove the tendons of his arms and legs, hide them in a cave and set a dragon to guard them. At this crucial moment Zeus's crafty son, **Hermes**, managed to steal them back, helped his father put them back in place, revive his strength and hunt down his antagonist. While Zeus hurled an unending volley of lightning bolts at Typhon, his blood ran in rivers over the Thracian mountains (subsequently called the **Aimos** mountain range) and finally fled to Sicily, where Zeus buried him under Etna, the active volcano.

So ends the war between gods and divine beings, and the coming into being of a new order of things, with the **Greek Pantheon** presiding unchallenged throughout Ancient Greek mythology.

THE CREATION OF MAN

Many are the myths and many their variations that deal with the creation of man. According to Hesiod, the time of Cronos's reign was the **Golden Race** which led a paradisiacal life. There followed the **Silver Race** which wasn't quite as happy because evil, illegality, murder had entered the world, along with disrespect for the gods, who finally destroyed them. Then came the **Bronze Race** among whom first appeared weapons, violence, wars, sickness, and which destroyed itself. After that came the **Heroic Race** whose shining achievements were beneficial to man. And, finally, the **Iron Race** who, though their daily lives are a hard struggle for survival, are not without joy, love and hope.

Top: The goddess Athina giving life to the first humans, watched by Prometheus. Christian Griepenkerl. 1839 – 1916. Bottom: The same theme in a Roman relief. 3rd C. A.D. Louvre, Paris.

The most commonly accepted myth of man's creation is, however, is that after the Battle of the Titans, the gods fashioned all living things out of clay and other materials, baking them with fire. After that they bade the Titaness Iapetus, one of the Oceanides, **Prometheus** and **Epithimeus** to endow them with gifts to aid their survival. Epithimeus, though wise, started with the animals, providing them with all necessary means for them to prosper and

***Plato** described a creature, spherical in shape, which had at one and the same time three sexes: masculine, feminine and something sharing elements of both. These creatures were, however, so arrogant in their strength that Zeus decided to divide them into two, which is why, ever since then, people have felt that they were incomplete and strove through love to unite with their other half.*

multiply. But when he came to man he had already exhausted his supplies thus leaving him naked and defenceless.

PROMETHEUS THE BENEFACTOR OF MAN

Epithimeus's brother, **Prometheus**, unable to bear this injustice, took humankind under his protection and decided to endow them with **knowledge** and **fire**. This daring plan, which he knew that the immortals would disapprove of, he carried out, sneaking into Hephaestos's workshop, stealing his fire, giving it to man and teaching him its uses. At the same time he handed on to them a lot of other knowledge and, thus equipped, they developed the arts and their cultural lives, escaping from their primitive state and achieving great things. Zeus's rage was terrible when he discovered what had happened and he devised the most terrible way of punishing Prometheus he could devise: After chaining him to a mountainside in the **Caucuses** he sent an *eagle* to feed every day to feed on Prometheus's liver, which every night grew back again (a feature

Top: The torture of Prometheus. Grigory Karpovich Mikhailov. 1814 – 1867.
Centre: Prometheus giving fire to man. Heinrich Friedrich Fueger. 1817.
Bottom: Heracles releasing Prometheus. Christian Griepenkerl.

Top: Prometheus stealing fire from Olympus. Christian Griepenkerl. Centre: Pandora's box. Dante Gabriel Rosseti. 1828 – 1882.

of this organ known in ancient times) to be again consumed. This martyrdom lasted thirty years, until **Hercules**, passing by on his search for the Garden of the Hesperides, slew the eagle, broke the chain and set Prometheus free. As a way of showing his gratitude, he showed Hercules the way to the Garden and told him that he would encounter his brother **Atalanta** who would help him to get the **Apple of the Hesperides** (see the chapter about Hercules).

This great benefactor of mankind finally gained immortality, but in a strange way. The wise and immortal centaur **Cheiron** was once wounded so badly that he couldn't bear the pain and begged Zeus to take away his immortality and grant it, instead on Prometheus, who thus took his place among the immortals.

Heracles killing the eagle sent to torture Prometheus. Attic krater, 6th C. B.C.

PANDORA

In most of the most ancient myths, man is created first, then woman. Hesiod says that the first mortal woman was created by **Hephaestos** - from earth and sea – and was named **Pandora**, on account of the fact that she was endowed with every gift ("dora", in Greek) including beauty, grace, sweetness, persuasiveness, perceptiveness, intelligence and, generally, all the positive elements of womankind. However, after that,

Hera added curiousity and Hermes craftiness and lies to the endowment.

Zeus sent **Epimitheas** to Pandora as a gift and, won by her charms, he married her. At the wedding, along with other gifts, Pandora was given a beautiful gilt box by the immortals, locked, with a key, and she was commanded never to open it, if she wanted to remain completely happy. So the couple lived many years together, in bliss, until Pandora's curiousity got the better of her and she opened the box. What flew out from it were all the misfortunes of the world: sickness, pain, calamity and whatever else. The last to emerge, however, was a little bird, **hope**, which gives solace and courage to mankind.

From that myth has come the phrase "to open **Pandora's box**", used when someone acts without reckoning the consequences.

PYRRHA AND DEUCALION

The myth of the Great Flood, founded on actual events, is recorded in the collective memory of humankind and recurs in many mythologies around the world, such as those of the Greeks, the Indians, the Mayas, the Aztecs and the Jews of the Old Testament.

According to Greek myth, man had become so wicked, disrespectful and unjust that Zeus decided to send a great flood to wipe them from the face of the earth. Amongst them, however, were the royal family of Thessalia, **Deukalion** – Prometheus's son – and **Pyrrha**, daughter of Epithimeas and Pandora, who were just and good. So Prometheus gained Zeus's permission to advise his son to build a great wooden boat – the arc in which Deucalian stowed everything necessary for survival, as well as animals

Centre: Pandora. Waterhouse.
Bottom: Hephaestos creating Pandora.
Attic vase, the work of Cleophon, 430 B.C.

and, together with Pyrrha, shut themselves in to await the storm.

The deluge lasted nine days and nights, flooding the creation and wiping out every trace of man. When, at last, the rain stopped and the waters began to recede, the Arc ran aground on the peak of Mount **Parnassos**. Immediately after leaving the arc the couple made sacrifice to the gods, thanking them for their salvation. In appreciation of their piety, Zeus sent Hermes to ask them whatever favour they wanted. They answered "human beings" and Zeus was not loath to comply, hoping for a better, new generation.

He sent instructions that they should walk forward with covered faces, throwing stones behind them, without looking round. From the stones that Pyrrha threw, women sprung, while from those of Deucalion, men. So was a new generation of human beings created.

*Pyrrha and Deucalion had their own children. Their first-born son, **Ellinus**, became the first ancestor of all the Greeks (**Ellinon**), gave his name to the country (**Ellada**) and the different Greek tribes were named after his descendents. From his son **Dorus** came the **Dorians**, from **Aiolos** the **Aiolians**, while from his grandsons, Ion and **Achaios** came the Ionians and the **Achaians**.*

*Their daughter **Pandora** (grand-daughter of the first Pandora) gave birth to **Grekos**, who gave his name to the priests at Dodona, the **Grekoi** which afterwards was used in the west as their name for Hellada, **Greece**. Another of their daughters, **Thoia**, gave birth to a daughter, **Magne**, first ancestor of the **Magnesians**, and a son, **Macedonas**, founder of the **Macedonians**.*

Top: Deucalion and Pyrra throwing stones that metamorphose into children. Virgil Solis. 1652.
Bottom: Deucalion's flood. Johann Heinrich Schonfeld. 1609 – 1684.

THE OLYMPIAN GODS

ZEUS

HER

ATHINA

POSEIDON

APHRODIT

APOLLO

DEMETER

ARE

ARTEMIS

HEPHAESTUS

IONYSUS

HERME

THE OLYMPIAN GODS

After the primitive myths of the creation and the first gods, with their terrible wars, a refined system of divine order came into being presided over by the **Twelve Olympian Gods** as well as other minor deities. The Olympians dwelt in a splendid shining palace on Olympos, the highest mountain in Greece, eating **ambrosia**, which rendered them invulnerable, and drinking **nectar** while receiving the smoke of sacrificed animals or of fruit, burnt on their alters. Human sacrifice was rare in Greece.

They were, in appearance, human, but on a larger dimension and with supernatural powers. Even though each of them was all-powerful, this was only within his own sphere, not impinging on those presided over by other deities. The gods swore by the "**water of Styx**", the sacred spring, a binding oath. Among other attributes, they had, as we have said, all of the virtues and vices of man, with whom they were continually in contact and whose lives they influenced up to a point.

It is on this point that there is a difference between Greek mythology and those of other ancient peoples: Man has his own free will, raised above and liberated from the primitive state, not merely a plaything of the gods or of fate, but created with freedom of spirit and action. The gods protected, aided, revenged and punished man; fearsome but also playful, loving man, joining with him to produce demi-gods (humans with super-human powers) and, generally, present at all of his actions.

A special god was assigned to every need, task, feeling or abstract idea, even if just to amuse. Generally there was a freshness, lightness and gracefulness about both the gods and the myths associated with them. Let's start our exploration, then, with the wonderful **Greek Pantheon**.

DIAS OR ZEUS

Middle: Head of Zeus. Roman copy of Greek bust of 5th C. B.C. Archaeological Museum, Rome.

Below: Zeus, with his two symbols of power: the eagle and lightning. Athenian amphora. 5th C. B.C. Louvre, Paris.

The ancient name for Dias was **Zeus**. The name Dias derives from the Indo-European root-word **Dyes**, from which came the Greek "Theos" and the Latin "Deos".

He is the chief god of the Pantheon, father of the gods and of man. From his palace on Olympos he reigns over the whole cosmos, the gods and man, with his terrible weapons, **thunder** and **lightning**. The areas over which he held sway, attached to his name, were numerous: Zeus supreme, **Nefeliyeretis** (the cloud-shifter), he who is called upon by mortals and by whose name they swear (**Oath-giving** Dias), he who preserves balance in the order of things, protector of cities, daily social life, of unwritten laws and of institutions (**Agoraios**), protector also of the family (**Erkios** Dias), refugees and asylum-seekers (**Ikesios**) and foreigners in general (**Xenios** Dias), - hospitality being considered sacred in Ancient Greece and governed by special laws.

When Zeus was born, his mother, Rhea, hid him in a cave on **Mount Ida** in Crete (see chapter: Cronos and Rhea).When he grew up he seized power from his father, after the Battles of the Titans and of the Giants and became chief of the

gods, after sharing areas of power with his brothers, sisters and children who had aided him in the wars.

His love life was so rich that we can only refer here to the most important ones, or those for whom he had the most passion. Let's start with his wives.

It is said that his first wife was **Mytis**, who bore him the goddess **Athina** (see relevant chapter). The second was **Dioni**. They were worshipped together at the sanctuary of Dodona in Epirus. The third was **Themis**, who personified Justice and was portayed blindfolded, with scales in her outstretched hand. She gave birth to the **Hours**, **Evnomos** (order), **Justice**, **Peace** and the **Fates**. But his most legal, faithful and well-known wife was his sister, Hera, who gave birth to **Ares**, **Hephaistos**, **Ivi** (goddess of eternal youth) and **Eileithyia** who aids women in childbirth.

Centre: The Goddess Ivi. Charles Durand. 1837-1917.

Zeus provoked Hera's jealousy and anger with his continuous erotic adventures, which often had unpleasant but sometimes humorous outcomes.

Among his innumerable lovers we will refer, in short, to the most important, together with the children they had. As is usually the case, they are also involved in other myths.

With **Dimitra**, another of his sisters, he fathered **Persephone**, with **Mayia**, **Hermes**, with **Semele**, **Dionysos**, with **Lytto**, **Apollo** and **Artemis**, with **Mnemosyni** the **nine Muses**, with **Evrinomi** the **Three Graces**, with

Zeus and Hera. Detail. James Barry, 1741 – 1806.

Top right: Zeus as a satyr and Antiope. Mosaic.

Alkmeni, **Hercules**, with **Leda** the **Dioskouroi** and **Helen** of **Troy**, with **Danae**, **Perseus**, with **Tayigete**, **Lacedaimon** and innumerable others. But apart from the hundreds of adventured he had with women, mortal and immortal, he also fell in love with a handsome prince of Troy, **Ganymede** by name, who he abducted and carried off to Olympos to have him close by his side as a wine-server.

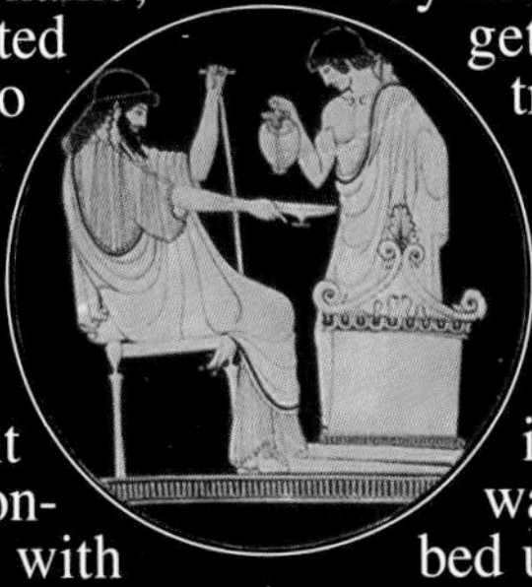

Among the most important of Zeus's relationships is that with Europa, which requires a section to itself.

The Abduction of Europe

The European continent was named after the beautiful young daughter of the king of the Phoenicians, **Agenor**, and his wife **Telephassa**, her brothers being Cadmus, Kylix an Phoenix.

When Zeus caught sigh of her wandering in th fields with her friends h was immediately smitte by her and, in order t get close to he transformed him self into a beauti ful white bul Europe, draw by the lovel animal, stroke it and, since was so tame, clim bed up on its back. A that moment the **bull-Zeu** took off and gallope through the sky with th speed of lightning, passin over land and sea until h reached Crete where the

Centre: Zeus and Ganymede. Attic Kylix. 480 B.C. Paul Getty Museum, California. Bottom: Zeus and Aegina. Attic lekythos. 450 B.C. Boston Museum.

nade love and had three ;ons: the legendary **Minos**, **Rhadamanthus** and **Sarpedon**.

When Zeus returned to Olympus (…and Hera) he took care to reinstate Europe by marrying her to the King of Crete, **Asterion**, so that her children would have a mortal father to look after them. After Asterion's death, Minos and Rhadamanthus ruled in Crete (see chapter on the Myths of Crete) while Sarpedon, expelled from Crete by Minos, went to Asia Minor, was made king of the Lycians and worshipped as a god. Europe spen the rest of her life ir Crete, while the brother and sisters that her father sen to fetch her back and, failing, neve dared to return tc their homeland founded kingdoms in a number of places: **Kylix** in **Kylikia**, **Phoenix** in **Phoenicia**, **Cadmus** in **Theban Cadmeia** (see relevant chapters).

Zeus was worshipped throughout Greece (**pan-**

LEDA AND THE SWAN

*Zeus once desired **Leda**, the wife of King Tyndareus of Sparta. In order to get access to her he metamorphosed into a beautiful **swan** that, she enfolded in her embrace. From their union were born the famous twins, the **Dioscuroi** and the beautiful **Helen**.*

Top: Leda and the Swan. Roman mosaic from Paphos. 3rd C. .D. Levcosia Museum. Bottom: Europa and the bull. Mosaic from Pompeii. Archaeological Museum, Naples.

Top, left: Graphic representation of the gold and ivory statue of Zeus at Olympia. Work of Phidias.

Hellenic Zeus), every city making sacrifices to him and holding ceremonies held in his honour. But his most important sanctuaries were at **Dodona**, which was the oldest, and at **Olympia**. At Dodona was the famous **Oracle of Zeus** (see chapter of Oracles), while at Olympia was his greatest temple, with the gold and ivory statue of him by **Phidias** (one of the Seven Wonders of the ancient world) and, of course, the **Olympic Games**, the most important of all those in Greece, were held there, in his honour every four years. In addition there was the Macedonian city of **Dion**, close to Olympus and dedicated entirely to the greatest of its gods. Outside Greece, there were important sanctuaries in Lybia (**Ammon-Zeus**) and at **Pergamon**. One of the largest temples dedicated to him was the famous Olympion, in Athens, known today as **the columns of Olympian Zeus**.

The sacred bird, symbol of Zeus (as well as lightning) was the royal **eagle**. Also, in order to honour the goat, Amalthia, that had given suck to him when he was young, he bestowed on its horn the property of being always full of everything that is bountiful, so that it became the symbol of fruitfulness and plenty, the **Cornucopia**.

Left: Bronze statue of Zeus hurling a thunderbolt. Classical period. Archaeological Museum, Athens.

HERA

Daughter of Cronos and Rhea, sister and wife to Zeus, she is the guardian of women, married life, legitimate children and, together with her daughter, **Eileithyia**, of childbirth.

She was legendary for the jealousy she showed to the, admittedly, unending infidelities of her husband as well as her vengefulness towards his lovers and their illegitimate children. Her rage against Hercules cost him many trials.

Her birthplace (in spite of the fact that she had been vomited out of Cronos's stomach, along with other gods) was located in Argos or Samos.

She fell in love with Zeus when they met, for the first time, in a remote part of **Mount Kithairon**, where Zeus had taken on the form of a cuckoo to protect himself from the rain. Together they parented **Ares**, **Ivi**, **Eileithyia,and**, finally, **Hephaestos**, who was born prematurely, after a difficult delivery. The child was so ill-proportioned that when Hera saw him she hurled him out of Olympus in disgust. Landing on Limnos, he was brought up by the inhabitants until the time was ripe for him to take his

Top, right: Hera tied to her throne with invisible bonds. Detail from vase.
Centre: Hera Ludovisi.
Roman statue, 1st C. A.D. Rome.
Bottom: Zeus and Hera: Agostino Garacci, 1557 – 1602.

Hera, growing weary of Zeus's unfaithfulness, once thought of leaving him and took refuge in Evoia, turning a deaf ear to his pleas. The wise ***Cithairon*** *advised Zeus to dress a xoana (wooden statue) in bridal clothes to make it look as though he were remarrying.*
When Hera learned of this she returned hotfoot and, tearing aside the veil understood the trick that had been played on her by Zeus and his love for her, turning her frown to smiles. And so they were reconciled.

rightful place on Olympus.
The goddess is portrayed, in sculptures and on vases as being very beautiful and noble, her crown being the symbol of her power. Other symbols associated with her are the cuckoo, peacock, scepter, pomegranate (symbol of fertility) and the lily.
Her worship was widespread in Greece, centring on **Argos** – where they celebrated her wedding with Zeus, in **Evia**, **Olympia** and in **Samos** where they held celebrations in honour of **Hera** and **Kallisteia** and the **Hecatomb**. On Samos was the most important of the temples dedicated to Hera, the famous **Heraion**.

Above, right: Scene of Heracles's ascent of Olympus. Athina is presenting the hero to Zeus while Hera pointedly looks away.
Centre: View of the Temple of Hera on Samos.
Bottom left: The Battle of the Giants: Hera and t he giant Phoitos.
Attic kylix 4th C. B.C. Berlin Archaeological Museum.

POSEIDON

The ruler of the seas – or **Pelagaios** – was Zeus's brother and the son of Cronos and Rhea. As one of the ruling twelve gods he dwelt sometimes on Olympus and sometimes in his wonderful palace in the depths of the sea, with his wife, the Nereid **Amphitritis** and his son, **Triton** (a prominent sea deity). Following Zeus's example, he led an active love-life, fathering many children with his numerous lovers. Together with **Alia**, he had six sons and one daughter, **Rodi**, after whom Rhodes was named. He was also considered to be the father of the hero **Theseus** (see relevant chapter).

It was he who first tamed the horse, created the winged horse **Pegasus** and the **Gorgons**. Traveling over the waves in his golden chariot around which the dolphins played, he was able to conjure up storms or to calm them through the power of his **trident** – gift of the Cyclops. He is the guardian of sailors and fishermen.

The dispute he had with Athina over the lordship of Athens is well-known (see chapter: Athena) as is the grudge he enmity he felt against **Odysseus** which caused him to wander the seas for

Top: Poseidon. Roman mosaic, 3rd C. A.D.
Centre: Statue of Poseidon. Copenhagen, 2005
Bottom: Poseidon's return. John Singleton Copley, 1738 – 1815.

Top: Poseidon and Amphitrite. Jacob de Gheyn, 1565 – 1629. Centre: Poseidon in the form of a bull and Amphitrite. Roman mosaic.

ten years. In addition to the trident, his symbols are: fish, sea-horses, dolphins and bulls.

He was the patron-god of Corinth, where they celebrated the **Poseidonia**, of **Thebes** and of many Greek colonies, since it was considered that he had assited in their foundation.

He was also honoured by horse races, held throughout Greece, and in Crete by the **Tavrokathapsia**, (acrobatic bull-capturing games) the most important of their celebrations. One of the most beautiful temples dedicated to him is at **Sounion**, in Attica.

Bottom: Poseidon's horses. Walter Crane, 1845-1915. New Gallery. Munich.

ATHINA

According to the prevailing myth, when Zeus had come of age in Crete, he fell in love with the wisest of the Oceanides, **Mytis**, whose advice helped him overcome Cronos. Perhaps she was his first wife. But it was prophecied that the daughter they would produce would be superior to her father in courage and wisdom. The frightened Zeus asked **Gaia's** advice who, in order to avoid future disputes, gave him a herb which shrunk the pregnant Mytida to such microscopic proportions that she could easily be swallowed. But things didn't stop there; Mytis wisely forestalled him, transplanting the embryo into his head.

As this strange pregnancy was reaching its end the god began to be racked by terrible, headaches which made him howl and thrash about so much that all Olympus quaked and trembled. Unable to take any more, he asked his son, **Hephaistos**, to strike him on the head to relieve him of the pain. When this was done out sprung a beautiful girl, with a warlike cry, fully-armed and terrible in her majesty. This was the goddess **Athina**, who had inherited the strength of her father and the wisdom of her mother. The birth of Athina is wonderfully portrayed on the East Frieze of the Acropolis (New Museum of the Acropolis).

Despite being a warlike deity, she wasn't a war chief because her character was a combination of strength and bravery with prudence, wisdom and intelligence. When Zeus saw her he was pacified and came to love her, she becoming his greatest ally, standing by him at the most difficult mo-

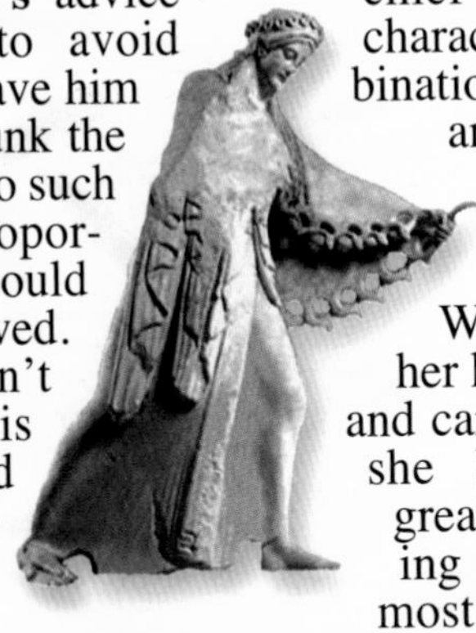

Top right: Reproduction of the statue of Athina in the Parthenon, Athens.
Centre: Athena. Detail from the Battle of the Giants. East freeze of the Parthenon. New Acropolis Museum, Athens.
Bottom: Athena springing from the head of Zeus. Attic kylix, 560 B.C.

Top right: The contest between Poseidon and Athena for the city of Athens. Athena's olive-tree offering.
Centre: Athena with her shield and helmet. Attic lekythos of 470 B.C. Work of Niconas. Massachusetts Museum.

ments. In recognition of the help she gave him in the Battle of the Giants, she was named the **first god** of the twelve. Generally, however, she is known as the goddess of **Wisdom**.

Every year the Athenians organized the great **pan-Athenaic** celebration in tribute to their patron-goddess. A grand procession, comprising the youth of the city, wound its way to the **Parthenon** on the sacred rock of the Acropolis, dedicated to the **Virgin Athina**. (she was always to remain a virgin), which is now the most important building on UNESCO's world-heritage list. A woolen chiton (garment) was offered to the wonderful gold-and-ivory statue that had been created by Phidias. (The first statue of her, made of wood, was to be found in the Erechthion). A special element in this celebration

Athena once found herself in opposition with **Poseidon** over the patronage of the city of Athens . In the most ancient myths Athina was called "**Cecropia**" after the first king of Athens , Cecrops. In the ensuing dispute, all of the Olympian gods, King Cecrops and the citizens of Athens acted as judges. First Poseidon struck the rock of the Acropolis with his trident, creating a **spring** of salt water which, because Athens is close to the sea, hardly made an impression. Then he made a beautiful horse to emerge which, however, did not sway the judges. But when Athena presented to the city an **olive tree** – symbol of peace and prosperity – they unanimously awarded her the prize. Athena took Athens under her protection, was always given the highest honour, and named the city after her.

Above: Statue of Athena outside the Austrian parliament building, Vienna.
Top right: Arachne metamorphosed into a spider.

was that the youth of Athens wore in their hair a golden cicada, another symbol of the city and its goddess.

But the main symbol of Athina was the **owl**, the bird of wisdom, representations of which were found all over the city, dedicated to the goddess. Her nickname "**Glafkopis**", was derived from the Ancient Greek name for this bird (**Glaux**). The Athenians had, and still use an expression: "komizei glaukus es Athinas", which is the equivalent of "To carry coals to Newcastle."

Apart from being known as The Virgin, Athina had many titles which display

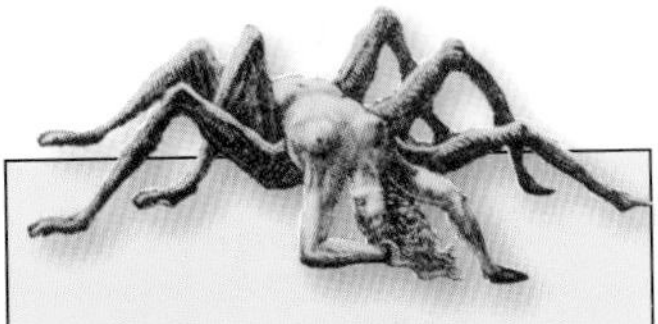

Both the remorseless and the pitying side of the goddess's character, is shown in the myth of ***Arachne****, an accomplished weaver who made the mistake of boasting that she was superior to anyone in this skill. So Athina challenged her to a weaving contest.*

Her tapestry showed her dual with Poseidon, while that of her rival the loves of the gods. Driven furious by this affrontery, Athina tore her rival's tapestry to pieces and Arachne hanged herself out of shame. At which the goddess, feeling sorry for her, gave her life again as a spider constantly spinning its thread.

Top right: Statue of Athena. Roman copy of a Greek original of the 5th C. B.C. Capitoline Museum, Rome

not only her attributes but her valour. She is known as **Athina of the City**, as the protector of Athenian society, **Pallada**, because she killed the Giant of that name, **Promachos** ("bastion") because of her support for the Athenians in war, **Areia** ("of the Court") because she presided over the High Court at the trial of Orestes (see relevant chapter) and **Ergani** ("erga" = work) because she was the patroness of the arts and also worked together with Hephaistos. She also guarded and aided many heroes, chief of which were Hercules and Perseus, was always at the side of the wily Odysseus and actively intervened on the side of the Greeks in the Trojan War. Apart from the owl her symbols were the olive tree and all of her armouring (which she is always shown wearing): spear, helmet and her famous shield.

Athina was worshipped in various parts of Greece, such as on the **Tenero** peninsula in South Lakonia and on the island of **Egina**, at the important temple of **Athina Aphaias**. Her worship was carried over into the Roman Pantheon under the name of **Minerva**.

Centre: Athena offering Heracles some wine. Attic kylix, 490-470 B.C. Archaeological Museum, Munic.
Bottom: The contest of Athena and Poseidon for the land of Attica. Reconstruction of Acropolis west pediment. (437-432 B.C.)

DEMETER

Daughter of Cronos and Rhea, she was one of the most ancient divinities that were worshipped. From her name was derived the word **dimitriaka** ("grain, crops"). She is the goddess of agriculture and of farmers as well as of wild plants and the fertility of the earth.

Her loves were few: first, Zeus, her brother, with whom she had her beautiful daughter, **Persephone**; then, her other brother, Poseidon, with whom she gave birth to another daughter, **Despina**, (whose name it was forbidden to utter to any but the initiates of the Elevsinian Mysteries). Finally, she fell in love with the Titan, **Iasion**, with whom she coupled in a thrice-ploughed field, and gave birth to **Plutos**, giver of wealth and plenty.

The Abduction of Persephone

When the god of the Underworld, **Pluto**, saw Persephone, he fell deeply in love with her and carried her off to his kingdom of Hades, where he married her and made her its queen. In her pain and despair at her daughter's absence, Demeter began to wander the earth, in an attempt to find out where her daughter had gone and neglecting her duties. The earth ceased to be fruitful, leading to great misfortune. When she learned the truth, from Helios, she threatened not to let anything grow on earth for as long as her daughter was absent. At this, Zeus commanded Pluto, to return the maid to her mother, which he was obliged to obey. On the way back, however, he gave her a pomegranate

Top right: The abduction of Persephone. Gian Lorenzo Bernini. 1622. Hamburg
Centre: Head of Demeter.
Bottom left: The return of Persephone from Hades. John Leighton, 1891.

***Triptolemus**, prince of Elevsina, favoured by the goddess Dimitra, was connected with the cultivation of cereals. The goddess presented him with a chariot heaped with wheat and harnessed to winged dragons so that he could go all around the world teaching people about cultivation. The goddess initiated him into her worship and he became her high priest and the **hierophant** of the **Elevsinian mysteries**. There was to be found an altar to him as well as the threshing-floor on which, according to legend, he threshed the first corn.*

Top right: Demeter and Triptolemus. Krater, 480 B.C. Carlsburg, Germany. Bottom: Representation of the Elevsinian Mysteries.

seed to eat, which transgression forced her to return to him. In the end, though, a solution was found: she would spend four months of the year with her husband (the unfruitful winter months) and the remaining eight with Demeter, who brings bounty to the earth and makes it blossom.

Demeter's symbols are: an ear of corn, the narcissus, myrtle, crocus and her sacred bees. The greatest celebration of the goddess was the pan-Helladic **Thesmophoria**, in which only women took part, pleading for the fertility of the earth. Her most important sanctuary was at Elevsis where, every year, the renowned **Elevsinian mysteries** were held, thus named because certain secret rituals took place in the sanctuary, administered by the

Top right: Hecate and Hermes aiding Persephone to return to her mother, Demeter. Attic krater of the Classical period.

Ierophantes, (holy priests of the goddess). In order to participate, a candidate had to be initiated into the mysteries; that is, to become an Initiate of the worship of Demeter. These **Initiates** were bound on oath never to reveal anything about the rituals to anyone. For that reason we have absolutely no information about what actually happened.

The Athenians would go there in a magnificent procession, following the **Sacred Road**, strewn with fruit and flowers, while during the whole period of the Mysteries truces were called and wars stopped. Even more archaic celebrations in honour of Demeter were the **Dimitria** and the **Dendrophoria**, renowned fertility celebrations that were first held at Elevsina and then transferred elsewhere.

A very primitive and strange custom of agricuturalists in antiquity is that after they had ploughed the land they sowed it with clay models of spermatozoa, in this way appealing to Dimitra to give fertility of the earth. Though quite a few examples of these have been found on excavations the answer to the intriguing question as to how they knew, without the aid of microscopes, what sperm looked like, has not yet been answered.

Centre: The goddess Demeter. Roman copy of a Greek original from the Classical period. Vatican, Rome.
Bottom: Hades and Persephone enthroned. Relief, 5th C. B.C.. Museum Magna Graecia, Petzio, Calabria.

APHRODITE

The goddess of beauty and love was not only the most beautiful of the Olympians but the most beautiful creature in the world, awakening love and desire in gods and mortals.

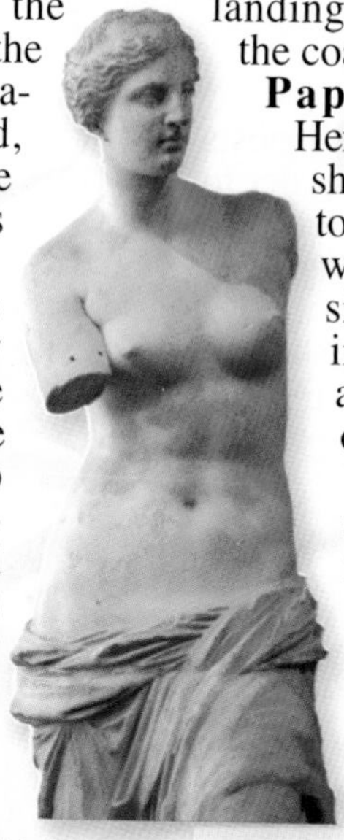

According to the most commonly accepted myth she was born from the foam whipped up when Cronos castrated Uranus and threw his genitals into the sea. So she emerged from the white sea foam (from which she takes her name) naked and shining on a white shell drawn by doves. The balmy Zephyrus wind bore her to **Kythira**, which was considered to be her particular island, where the first of her sanctuaries was to be found. Afterwards she journeyed to **Cyprus**, landing on the coast at **Paphos**. Her worship spread to all of the island, where she was considered the most important goddess and given the title of "Kypris".

The goddess had a rich love-life. Her most important relationship was with the god **Ares**. Her husband, **Hephaestos**, who she married subsequent to

Top right: Aphrodite and the swan. Attic kylix found in Kameiros, the work of Pystoxenos, about 460 B.C. British Museum, London.
Centre: The Venus de Milo. Louvre, Paris
Bottom: The birth of Venus. Sandro Botticelli, 1483. Uffizi, Florence.

Hephaestus surprises the lovers. Julius Schnorr von Carosfeld, (1794 – 1872).

pressure from Zeus and Hera, getting wind of the fact that while he was away at the workshop his wife was entertaining a lover in their connubial bed, forged an invisible metal net before leaving, as if for work. But when the two lovers met in love's throes, Hephaestos appeared and, after he had cast his net and pinned them, naked, down, called for the other gods to hear his complaint and to mock the lovers. The gods were, indeed, very entertained by this piquant episode but also helped to find a way out, Poseidon taking the lead and promising that Ares would be punished. Aphrodite and Ares gave birth to **Deimus** and to **Phobos**, who were in the retinue of the god, and **Harmony** who awoke desire. Their most famous son, though, was the playful god, **Eros**.

Eros is portrayed as a beautiful, winged child with a bow and arrows with which he pierced hearts, awakening irresistible love, the only follower of Aphrodite.

Harmony, the daughter of this extra-marital match, created a balance between the goddess of love, symbolizing life, and the god of war, leading to death.

Centre: Adonis and Aphrodite. Antonio Canova, 1757 – 1822. Geneva. Bottom right: Adonis with his lyre. Attic lekythos, 400 B.C. Louvre, Paris.

Top right: Ares and Aphrodite. Mosaic from the House of Aphrodite, Pompeii. Centre: Scene from the Trojan War; Lycaon is trying to remove an arrow from Aeneas's knee, while his mother, Aphrodite, offers him some dictamos, the healing herb of Crete.

Aphrodite was love-stricken for the beautiful **Adonis**, in rivalry with Persephone, who was also smitten by him. The gods, as intermediaries, arranged that he should spend part of the time on Earth and part in the Underworld. When Adonis was killed, in a boar hunt, his blood gave rise to the first roses and Aphrodite's tears, anemones.

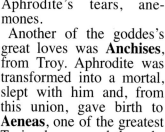

Another of the goddes's great loves was **Anchises**, from Troy. Aphrodite was transformed into a mortal, slept with him and, from this union, gave birth to **Aeneas**, one of the greatest Trojan heroes and the subsequent founder of Rome.

By **Dionyssos** she produced **Priapus**, a love god with huge genitals and a permanent erection. With Poseidon she gave birth to **Erica** and, according to one version, **Rodi** (who gave her name to Rhodes), while with Hermes, **Hermaphrodite**, a being with characteristics of both sexes.

One of Aphrodite's favourite games was to inspire Zeus with love for different mortals, thus enraging Hera, with whom her relationship was by no means good. She also helped lovers, even adulterers, but strictly punished whoever rejected offers of love. Attending on her, apart from Eros, were her

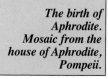

The birth of Aphrodite. Mosaic from the house of Aphrodite, Pompeii.

daughter, Harmony, the Hours, Ivi (goddess of youth), the three Graces and Peitho (Persuasion), who persuaded maidens to give themselves to love.

She took the side of the Trojans in the Trojan War, on account of the fact that Paris had awarded the apple on which was written "To the most beautiful." to her. (See chapter on the Trojan War.)

She was worshipped in **Kithira**, in **Cyprus**, at **Knidus** (Knidian Aphrodite) and elsewhere and had two titles showing different properties: **Uranian Aphrodite** (daughter of Uranus) was the protector of marriages, which is why new brides donated silver drachmas in special collection boxes as offerings to the goddess (*you can see such a box at the New Museum of the Acropolis*). **Pandimos**

Top right: Aphrodite bathing. Archaeological museum, Rhodes. Bottom: Aphrodite offering arms to Aeneas. Nicolas Poussin, 1639.

Aphrodite was the goddess of earthly, fleshly love, the invincible.

She is the only divinity who is portrayed naked in order to reveal her full beauty, something that in other deities would be considered disrespectful. There are numerous wonderful statues of her, the most important being the **Venus** de **Milo**, which is in the Louvre.

At an important temple dedicated to her on the **Acrocorinth**, the priestesses would let men pay to lie with them once a month as a contribution to the temple finances. From this practice comes the word **ierodoulos**" ("holy worker") which today is a euphemism for a prostitute. One of the goddess's responsibilities was, in fact, the protection of whores.

ARES

A legitimate son of Zeus and Hera, he belonged to the second generation of the Olympians and is the god of **war**, bloodthirsty, quick-tempered and aggressive. In spite of his manly beauty and his physical courage he was regarded with particular dislike by both gods and man and worshipped in just a few places, mainly by the Thracians, a war-loving race.

He often came into conflict with Athina, who was also a warlike divinity but who, as the goddess of wisdom and reasoning, knew how to get the better of him. His behaviour often enraged Zeus, who was obliged to bring him to trial for wanton murder, this trial being held on a rocky eminence ("pagos", in Ancient Greek) close to the Acropolis, in Athens, named the **Areos Pagos**, the first criminal court in the world. The Athenians gave this name (and do so still) to their highest criminal court. Ares was, in the end, declared innocent.

He was on the Trojan side in the Trojan War.

He had extra-marital affairs with **Aphrodite**, who was married to Hephaistos (see chapter on

Top right: The Borgese Ares, Roman copy of a Greek work from the Classical period, probably by Alcmenes. Louvre, Paris.
Centre: Ares and Aphrodite. Athenian kylix by Oltos.
Bottom right: Aphrodite and the three Graces arming Ares. David 1822.

Top right: Head of Ares. Roman copy – 2nd C. A.D. – of a Greek original of the 5th C. B.C.

Aphrodite for this racy episode). With Aphrodite he had five children, two of whom, **Phobos** and **Deimos** (personifications of "fear" and of "flight") were among his constant attendants, while the other three: Hemera, Eros and Harmony, took on the character of their beautiful, sensual mother. Harmony married **Cadmos**, the King of Thebes, which was thus one of the few places where Ares was worshipped.

Other of his daughters were the **Amazons**, war-loving women mounted on wild horses who had cut off one of their breasts to allow them easier use of the bow.

Other male-children of Ares include **Diomides**, the King of Thrace, with his terrible man-eating horse (see chapter on Hercules), the hero **Meleager**, **Drianta**, **Lykaona** and **Ennomus**.

His symbol was his terrible war – equipment, while, apart from Deimos and Fovos, his followers were **Enios** (another war deity) who served wine to him in his chariot, and **Eris**, the goddess of strife.

Centre: Scene from a theatrical performance; actors playing the parts of Hephaistus and Ares clash under Aphrodite's gaze. Bottom left: Ares, Aphrodite and Eros. Paris Bordone. 1560.

ARTEMIS

Another of Zeus's lovers was **Leto**. When Hera learned that she had become pregnant, the furious goddess persecuted her so much that she couldn't find anywhere to give birth and also prevented Eileithyia, her daughter, protector of pregnant women, from offering Leto assistance. After Leto had wandered through the whole of Greece in her search, Zeus asked Poseidon for help and he made appear **Delos** (dilos= make appear) a small, parched island, where Leto finally found sanctuary.

*The island of **Delos**, tied to the worship of Apollo, became, in historical times the holy island of all the Greeks, where, every year, ceremonies and music contests were held. It was forbidden – and still is – to stay overnight there or to die there. For this reason the seriously ill were taken to the nearby island of Rhinia.*

Without the aid of Eileithyia, however, the birth was extremely difficult; racked with pain for nine days she was still unable to give birth until **Iris**, learning the news, sped to the islet. It was then that Leto gave birth, first to **Artemis**, then, between an olive tree and a date palm, to **Apollo**.

Artemis is one of the most ancient, complex and interesting figures in the Greek Pantheon. She is the goddess of hunting, the moon, chastity and virginity (**Virgin Artemis**), because she asked her father to allow her never to marry or have children. The same chastity was required of her followers and priestesses. She

Centre: The Versailles Artemis. Copy of a work by Leocharis.
Bottom right: Leto and her children, Artemis and Apollo. Crater 470 B.C. Louvre.

was the protectress of hunters, herdsmen, tame and wild animals, forests and nature in general, as well as children, innocent juveniles, young virgins and the pregnant.

At her sanctuary at **Bravronas**, in Attica, they made offerings of the garments (chitons) of women who had died in pregnancy and childbirth.

Dressed always in a short chiton, with her bow and arrows, she spent most of her time wandering freely through the forest and countryside with her followers, the **Hamadryads** – nymphs of the forests and waters.

Restless, energetic, imperious, serious but inflexible in her decisions and severe in her punishment of those who failed to show her respect. One example of this is the punishment she handed out to **Alkaion**, a renowned hunter who chanced to come across her naked, bathing in a spring, and, after she had changed him into a deer, was torn to pieces by his fifty dogs, which she had driven mad.

Another victim was **Niobe**, daughter of Tantalus, who, in an unguarded moment, boasted that she had given birth to fourteen children, while Artemis had only two. Artemis, together with her brother, Apollo, vowed to avenge this insult and hunted down Niobe's children with bows and arrows, Apollo killing the boys and Artemis the girls.

Yet another victim of Artemis's inflexibility and harshness was the punishment afforded to one of her followers, **Callisto**, who, because she had broken her oath of chastity and had a child by Zeus, was changed into a bear. Zeus,

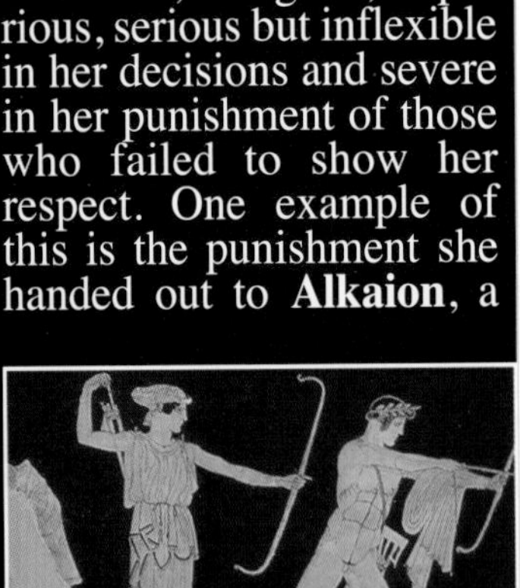

Centre: Artemis feeding a swan. Athenian lekythos, 5th C. B.C. Hermitage Museum, St Petersburg.
Bottom: Artemis and Apollo killing Niobe's children. Detail. Attic kalyx, about 450 B.C.

Top right: Artemis rescuing Iphigenia and leaving a deer in her place. Roman copy of a Classical Greek statue.

however, intervened, setting her in the night sky as the constellation of the **Great Bear**.

She took the side of the Trojans in the Trojan War, along with her brother, mainly because Agamemnon had killed her sacred deer. (see chapter on the Trojan War).

The symbols of the goddess were a variety of plants and animals, but chiefly the deer, as well as her bow, quiver and arrows (**Artemis of the Golden Bow**).

Her places of worship were Bravrona in Attica, where her sanctuary still stands, Anabissos in Attica and Ephesus on the Ionian coast of Asia Minor, the site of the **Artemision**, the magnificent, renowned temple of **Ephesian Artemis**, the construction of which took a hundred and twenty years. The giant statue of her inside the building, a masterpiece of Greek art, was created by Skopas (the base), Praxiteles (the altar) and the statue by Phidias, Miron and Polykleitos. This **temple**, one of the Seven Wonders of the World, was wholly destroyed in an act of arson. Statues of Artemis, in the eastern style, can be found in the Museum at Ephesus. The worship of Artemis was later adopted by the Romans, who called her **Diana**.

Bottom right: Artemis and Actaeon. Attic krater, 470 B.C. The Fine Arts Museum, Massachusetts.

APOLLO

One of the greatest and most loved of the Olympian gods, presiding over many areas: the God of **Light**, the sun, harmony, music, the arts in general, divination, healing, father of **Asclepius**, to whom he taught medicine (see chapter on Aclepius).

A child of Zeus and Leto, twin brother of Artemis, he was born on Delos. One of his titles - and he had at least three hundred - was **Delian**; that is, he who, shining, reveals everything. It was there on Delos that he had his first sanctuary.

One of the first of the young Apollo's acts was to search Greece for the best place for his worship. He found it in the foothills of **Mount Parnassus** at a place that was supposed to be the navel of the Earth, belonging to Gaia and protected by one of her sons, the huge snake, **Python**.

Apollo killed him with his bow and a flaming torch (**Pythian Apollo**) and, taking up residence, created his main centre of worship, **Delphi**, which, besides having his temple, also had the renowned **Oracle**, which played an important role in the whole of the Greek world (see chapter on the Oracle). On

Top right: Statue of Apollo outside the Academy of Athens. Leonidas Drosis, 1800.
Centre: Apollo making an offering. Pistoxenos, about 480 B.C.
Bottom: Apollo and the Python. Jan Boeckhorst, 1604 – 1668.

Top right: Daphne and Apollo. Jean Etienne Liotard, 1702 – 1789.

account of the varying prophesies issued by the God, he took the title **Loxias**. It was because of Apollo's eight-year banishment from Delphi, for his murder of Python, that the celebrations held in his honour, the **Pytheia**, were held every eight years.

As the god of music and harmony, he is always shown with the **lyre**, with which he accompanied both town and country dances.

He was the foe of barbarism and evil, teacher of the noble arts, notably of his son, **Orpheus**, who became the most accomplished of all musicians (see the myth of Orpheus and Euridice).

Because he was so handsome, the quintessence of youth and beauty, Apollo had many erotic adventures, the most notable of which was when he fell in love with the nymph, **Daphne**, who, however, wanting to keep her virginity, called on Gaia for aid, while he pursued her, and was turned into a laurel tree. In spite of his disappointment at the unfortunate outcome of his passion, Apollo made the laurel his sacred plant, and nearly always, in any representation of the god, he is shown crowned with a laurel wreath. In addition, the Delphic Sibyl chewed a laurel leaf before uttering a prophecy.

Bottom: Apollo seated on the sacred tripod at Delphi.

Top right: Apollo and the Muses on Parnassus. Anton Raphael Mengs. 1728 – 1779. Centre: The death of Hyacinth. Jean Brock. 1801.

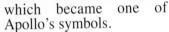

Another of Apollo's ill-fated loves was that for **Hyacinth**, a handsome Spartan prince who was also loved by Zephyr, the west wind, who, in his efforts to help Hyacinth escape from the god, killed him by hurling back the discus he had thrown on a gust of wind.

The sorrowful god transformed Hyacinth's body into the beautiful flower that still bears his name, which became one of Apollo's symbols.

The music contest between Apollo and **Marsyas**, who dared to challenge the god's musical supremacy, has a particular, horrible interest. The judges were the nine **Muses** (daughters of Zeus and Mnemosyne). As was to be expected, Apollo won the contest and punished the contender in a particularly gruesome fashion, flaying him alive. After that, the Muses became guardians of the Arts and were numbered among the god's following.

Left: Apollo and Hyacinth listening to Kyparissus playing the pipe. Alexander Ivanov.

Top right: The clash between Apollo and Hercules for possession of the sacred tripod. Lekani by Asteas, 350 B.C.
Centre: The music contest between Marsyas and Apollo.
Bottom: Sunrise. Apollo as Helios. Painting by Francois Bouchen (1703-1770).

Other sacred symbols of the god were the **lyre**, the **bow**, the **tripod**, a three-legged cauldron often used for offerings to the gods at Delphi, dolphins and gold, associated with him because of its closeness in colour to that of the sun.

Apart from Delphi and Delos, the god was worshipped in many other parts of Greece, where there were temples dedicated to him. Amongst them the temple of **Epicurean Apollo** at **Bassae** in Arcadia, in the Peloponnesus, one of the best-preserved temples in Greece and a UNESCO World Heritage site, the work of the architect Iktinos, who based it's design on the Parthenon.

The **Thargylia** celebrations in honour of the god and his sister, Artemis, were mainly to do with his healing powers, but also the purging of sins.

HERMES

The son of **Zeus** and **Maia**, daughter of Atlanta, from his childhood he was distinguished by his liveliness, quick-wittedness and craftiness, playing pranks on both gods and man, to their cost.

Extremely inventive, hardly had he been born than he broke out of his cradle and, coming across a tortoise, made the first lyre from its shell, which he later offered to Apollo in exchange for the title of protector of herds and herdsmen.

One of his main attributes was to be the **messenger** of the gods (like the less-important but more ancient divinity, Iris), undertaking to convey commands from gods to men as well as other confidential missions. One of his other functions was that of **Psychopompos**; that is, the leader of the souls of the dead to the **River Acheron**, where Chairon conveyed them to the Underworld.

He is the most sympathetic of the deities because, alongside his divine qualities, he has many human ones. The guardian of merchants and of trading, with his resourcefulness, quickness and cunning, he was the most Greek of the gods.

In addition he took care of travelers and roads. In classical times they erected **Columns of Hermes**, with

Bottom left: Hermes killing the giant, Argos, watched by Io metamorphosed into a cow. Peter Paul Rubens, 1636. Prado, Madrid.

*The giant **Argos**, the **all-seeing**, who had a hundred eyes, was the ever-vigilant watchman that **Hera** had assigned to watch over **Io**, the lover of Zeus who she had changed into a cow. Argos was killed by **Hermes**, at Zeus's behest, and Hera, set his hundred eyes on the tail of her sacred bird, the **peacock**, to honour him.*

Top left: Hermes with Aphrodite and Cupid. Nicolas Chaperon, 1612 – 1655.
Centre: The Hermes of Praxiteles. Archaeological Museum, Olympia.
Bottom: Hermes with his mother, Maya. Attic amphora, work of Nikoxenos, 5th C. B.C.

his head on them, as road signs, showing the main directions.

At the same time, he was the protector of mountebanks and thieves, taking great pleasure in the mayhem they caused. While still an infant, just as a prank, he stole the sacred cattle of Apollo who was obliged to use all his powers of divination to find out where they were hidden. Hermes managed to pacify the Angry Apollo by offering him the first lyre.

He is also considered to be the god of **luck** and, for that reason, whatever was found by chance on the road or elsewhere belonged to the god and was called **Ermaion**. They also attributed to him any unexpected stroke of luck or the sudden acquisition of wealth.

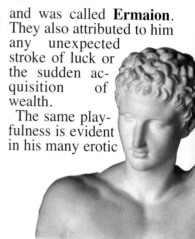

The same playfulness is evident in his many erotic adventures with beautiful nymphs. He joined with the goddess Aphrodite to produce **Hermaphrodite**, a human being with a blend of masculine and feminine characteristics. According to a myth, their beautiful son fell deeply in love with a nymph and, during a deep embrace, asked the gods never to part them, a plea the gods heeded, creating a double-natured being.

Hermes had many

children and among his descendants was the wily Odysseus.

The symbols of the god were his **winged sandals** and his winged hood which helped him to fly fast and the wallet. But the most important was the **Kyrikeio**, a wand entwined with two snakes which showed that he was the official messenger of Zeus and, in general, the bearer of commands from the immortals to men.

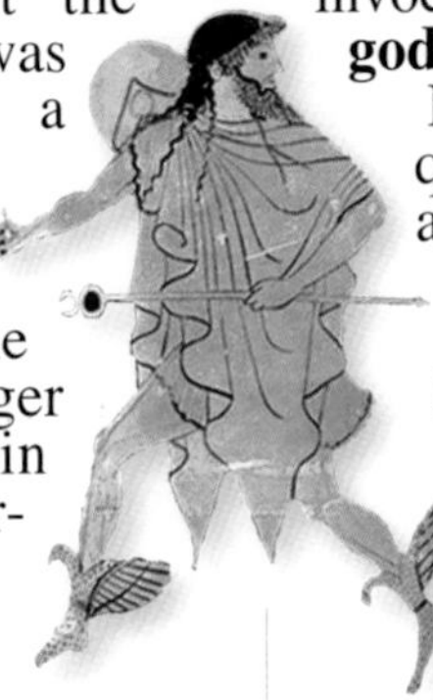

HESTIA

The eldest daughter of **Cronos** and **Rhea**, Hestia is the protectress of the **house** and of harmonious **family** life. Since every house had its own altar, with a lamp kept alight (the "hestia", from which she took her name) there were no special temples dedicated to this god. When a baby was born, the first thing the father did was to carry it round the **altar of Hestia**. At the start of the day, before they did anything else, people would make a small sacrifice at the altar, upon which oaths were also sworn. In general all sacrifices started with invocations to the **Hestian gods**.

Hestia was a serious, quiet goddess who always remained a virgin, in spite of the fact that both Poseidon and Apollo had asked for her hand in marriage.

In the centre of every town (usually at the prytaneum) was the navel of the town; that is the **public Hestia** on which the town's **sacred flame** was kept burning. Whenever a new city or colony was founded, the flame was sent to it, symbolizing the tie between them. At Delphi, the sacred flame of the goddess burnt constantly on the **Pan-hellenic Hestia**.

Top: Hermes. Athenian lekythus of the 5th C. B.C.
Bottom: The goddess Hestia. Attic Kylix, 5th C. B.C.

HEPHAISTOS

According to the prevailing myth about this son of Zeus and Hera, his mother had such a difficult delivery and, when he was born, he seemed so ugly to her, that she hurled him straight out of Olympus. Falling onto the island of **Lemnos**, he broke his leg and was forever after lame.

The Lemnians nurtured him and brought him up to be a blacksmith. Thus he became the god of fire and of **metal-working**, an unmatchable craftsman. He took the island under his protection, set up his workshop there and at the temple dedicated to him, the Lemnians taught his craft.

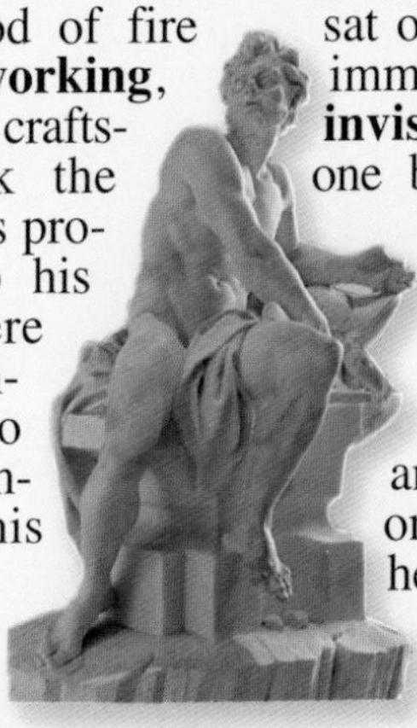

When he had grown up he decided to take revenge on his mother for the way she had behaved towards him. So he created a beautifully-crafted **throne** and sent it to her on Olympus as if as an offering. When Hera, attracted by its beauty, sat on the throne she was immediately tied by an **invisible bond** that noone but Hephaistos could untie. Only after much pleading by the gods did Hephaistos condescend to return to Olympus and untie the bond, but on the condition that he be given the goddess **Aphrodite** as his wife. The Olympians were shocked by the fact that this ugly and misshapen cripple wanted to marry the god-

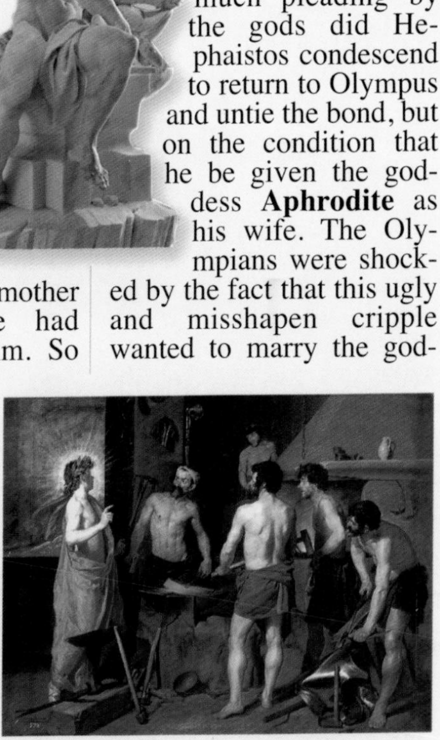

Right: Apollo visiting Hephaestus in his forge. Velazquez. 1630.

Top right: Thetis ordering Achilles' new weapons from Hephaestus. Attic amphora, 480 B.C.
Centre: Aphrodite in Hephaestus's forge. Louis le Nain, 1641.
Bottom: Hephaestus's return to Olympus. Hydria, 530 B.C.

dess of beauty. Aphrodite went wild with worry. But, after Hephaistos forged Zeus's thunderbolts, they gave way, allowing this mismatched couple to wed. Of course Aphrodite did not remain faithful to her husband and had a whole series of lovers. The episode in which he tied her and her lover, Ares, with invisible bonds is described in the chapter on Aphrodite.

Hephaistos's forges were to be found both on Lemnos and **Etna**, the Sicilian volcano (the Greek word for which, "*hephaestia*", comes from his name). It was there that he created the innumerable masterpieces for which he was renowned.

He created the shining **palaces** of the gods on Olympus (paying, of course, particular attention to his own), the scepter and lightning of Zeus, Apollo's shining chariot, all of the utensils and armaments of the gods (the arrows of Artemis and Apollo, Athena's golden buckle, Dionysos's silver cups) as well as Achilles' famous armour (the description of his shield in the Iliad is really wonderful) and Hercules' golden breastplate. The jewelry he created was of unmatchable beauty and fineness.

Apart from all these, he created the first moving **metal man** (a type of robot), **Talos**, one of his

Top left: Thetis watches Hephaestus making Achilles' new weapons. Mosaic from Pompeii. 1st C. A.D. Below: Attic red ground pelike, 530 B.C. Work of Cleophontas

gifts to **King Minos,** was a huge bronze giant who did a kind of sentry duty, walking around Crete three times a day.

Homer also mentioned that Hephaistos had bronze and gold helpers who could think, talk and had strength, working with him in the forge.

In addition he created the first woman, **Pandora**, out of clay as well as the terrible bonds of Prometheus.

His main place of worship was on Limnos, where the **Hephaistia** were celebrated yearly. Since he collaborated with Athina, he was especially worshipped in Attica as the protector of metalworkers – who used to hang a picture of him, along with that of Athina Erganis, in their workshops – the two of them being honoured at a yearly ceremony, the "Halkeia", held at the end of October. In the area of Athens' ancient market there is a beautifully preserved temple, the "Thyseion" (middle 5th C. B.C.) which is dedicated to Hephaistos.

In spite of being ugly and deformed, Hephaistos always kept company with beautiful women. Apart from Aphrodite, he had relationships with the beautiful **Chari** and **Aglayia**, the youngest and most graceful of the **three Graces**, by whom, of course, he had many children.

OTHER IMPORTANT GODS

PLUTO (HADES)

Although he is one of the main gods – the son of **Cronos** and **Rhea** and brother to Zeus and Poseidon – because he didn't reside on Olympos but in the **Underworld**, he isn't included in the Olympian Pantheon.

Aided by demons he ruled over the dead, who were forbidden to leave his kingdom. The only mortals ever to have entered Hades and returned did so under special conditions, associated with the romantic and heroic figures of Hercules, Orpheus, Theseus, Odysseus and Aeneus. (see relevant chapters)

The Underworld was a huge cavernous space surrounded by the **waters of the Styx** by which the gods swore their unbreakable oaths, the river **Acheron**, across which Charon ferried the souls of the dead, the fiery river **Pyriphlegethon**, and the river of pain and lamentation, **Kokyto**.

Centre: Hermes amidst the souls of Acheron, Adolf Hiremy-Herschl. Austrian Gallery, Vienna.

Hermes Psychopompos led the souls of the dead as far as the banks of **Lake Acheron**, where Chairon took over, asking one small coin called an **obolo** as payment for the crossing, a custom which continues in Greece right up to today.

At the end of the Acheron was **Cerberus**, a terrible monster in the shape of a three-headed dog, who

Left: The dead drink the waters of forgetfulness.

Top left: One of the rare representations of Pluto: the Abduction of Persephone. Niccolo dell' Abbate, 1537. Louvre. Paris.

Bottom left: Dionysus. Roman copy of a Greek statue of the 4th C. B.C.

prevented those who had entered Hades from leaving (see chapter on Hercules).

The Underworld was divided into four parts: the **Place of Judgement**, where the dead drank the **water of Lethe** (or forgetfulness) to forget the upper world and be judged for their acrions, **Purgatory**, where the souls of those who hadn't committed deadly sins underwent cleansing, **Tartarus**, the hell to which the souls of the unjust, criminals and suicides were led, and, finally, the **Elysian Fields** (Paradise), the only part of Hades where there was light; the place the good and the just continued to live happily.

Naturally, Pluto was not among those loved by both man and gods and for that reason there were neither sanctuaries nor temples devoted to him, men not being over-eager to meet him, while when they did sacrifice black animals to him, out of fear, every hundred year or so, they kept their heads turned and dug trenches so that the blood would soak to the depths of the earth.

DIONYSUS (BACCHUS)

The son of **Semele** and **Zeus**, Dionysus was a junior god in the Pantheion but one of especial importance, playing an important role in the religious life of Ancient Greece. An eternal youth, high-spirited, much loved by god and man, as the god of wine he traveled all over Greece teaching vine cultivation.

Dionysus was, strangely, born twice. The myth is as follows: catching wind of

Top right: Dionysus being born from Zeus's knee. Attic krater of the 5th C. B.C. Centre: Attic kylix, work of Macronas, 480 B.C. Bottom: Pentheus being torn apart by the Maenads. Kylix by Macronas from the 5th C.

the fact that Zeus was in love with Semele, daughter of Cadmus, Hera persuaded her to ask Zeus to reveal himself to her in all his godly majesty to prove his love for her. But when he granted her this favour, unable to withstand the dazzling light and the and lightning which shot from his hands, she was consumed by fire, after having given premature birth to Dionysus who was hidden by Gaia in some ivy. Understanding that the six-month old Dionysus had no chance of surviving, Zeus had him stitched into his thigh by Hermes, to mature for another three months, when he was reborn. Hermes, at the bid of Zeus, then transformed him into a goat and kept him hidden in a forest until he was grown up. But Hera's anger never abated and she obliged him to keep traveling through Greece and beyond, teaching the craft of viniculture.

The spirited god of wine was always accompanied by a clamorous, frenetic entourage, the **Bacchae** or **Meinads**, who after drinking themselves into a delirium abandoned themselves to orgiastic ceremonies.

Apart from the Meinads

*One myth refers to the opposition of **Pentheus**, the King of Thebes, to the promulgation of the worship of Dionyssus in his city, which was reckoned to be the birthplace of the god. In retribution the god lured him into the wild forests of Mount Citharon where his followers, the **Maenads**, tore him*

there were the **Satyrs**, half man, half goat, and the **Silini**, creatures with animal faces and horses' tails, all of which participated in his rites, singing, dancing and abandoning themselves to the most basic of instincts with the nymphs and mortals always to be found in his following, chief of whom was the god, **Pan** (see relevant chapter)

Strangely, this dizzy god who always had women as his chief companions in his unending celebrations, had few erotic adventures. But he was stricken with one of them; **Ariadne**, the daughter of Minos, and, after he had got Theseus drunk (see relevant chapter) put him into a deep sleep and implanted in him the idea of abandoning her on **Naxos**, where he, Dionyssus, could marry her. Afterwards he conveyed her to Olympus, to achieve immortality as the wife of a god, and to Naxos, to culture her worship as the guardian of the isle. Dionysus and Ariadne are portrayed on one of the most beautiful vases in the Archaeological Museum in Thessaloniki.

Their son, **Staphylos**, was the first to think of

Centre: Dionysus and a satyr. Attic Kylix by Macronas. Berlin.

Bottom right: Ariadne and Dionysus. Guido Reni, 1575 – 1642.

to pieces. Tragically at the head of this wild horde was Pentheus's mother, ***Agave****, who in her ecstatic madness mistook her son for a lion, wrenched off his head and stuck it on her thyrsis (wand) entwined with ivy.*

This story, and how Agave slowly came to realize the enormity of what she has done, is told in ***Euripedes's*** *gripping play "The* ***Bacchae****".*

mixing wine with water, though it was another Staphylos, a shepherd at the court of **Oineus**, the King of Calidon in Aetolia, who discovered the power of the grape, after observing that goats who ate the fruit of a previously unknown plant became more lively. He passed on this information to the king, who decided to try it himself and, after drinking the juice, felt refreshed and euphoric. So the fruit was named "staphili" and the juice "oinea", though, according to another version, it was Dionysus himself who discovered the vine's amazing properties.

The god Dionysus is always shown crowned with ivy or vine leaves, holding a bunch of grapes. His symbols are the ivy-twined staff, the thyrsus, and the phallus, which symbolizes the reproductive strength of nature.

On one of his journeys ***Dionyssus*** *was waylaid by a pirate ship heading from Tyre. Believing from his appearance that he was some rich nobleman, they seized him and took him on board, hoping to hold him for ransom. But suddenly the ship began to fill with wine, the mainmast became a vine, the god changed into a lion and the terrified crew, jumping overboard, were turned into dolphins.*

The **Dionysia** were celebrations held throughout Greece and its colonies abroad, the main centres being Athens, Corinth (later developing into the Pan-Helladic Isthmian Games), Boiotia, Naxos, Militos and Icaria.

The celebrations were joyful, worshippers being transported into exstatic states with the lavish consumption of wine, the playing of wild music, with drums and cymbals, and the display of phalluses. There were the Little

Centre: Dionysus in a pirates' ship, sprouting a vine while the pirates are turned into dolphins.
Bottom left: Dionysus battling with Indians. Roman mosaic. The Museum of Rome.

and the Great Dionysia. The Little ones were mainly wine harvest festivals, while the Great ones included sacrifices, processions and theatrical competitions.

Among other things, Dionysus was the god of the **Theatre**. Let's see, then, how theatre came to play a part in these celebrations. The god was especially honoured on the island of Icaria, where the **Dithyram**, a type of religious song in praise of him, originating with the poet **Ariona**, was cultivated. Together with the music he wrote lyrics and provoking or comic dialogues which were performed by men disguised in sheepskins and masks as **goatish Satyrs**. It was from this that the word "**tragedy**" originated (tragos = goat + odi = song). After this acted form of hymn reached Athens it underwent further transformations, evolving into the first theatrical performances in the world.

During the Great Dionysia, held in Spring, during the high Classical period (5th C. B.C.) the tragedies of the great poets were played – or, as they would say, "taught" - along with **comedies** and **satires**. The Athenian devotion to the theatre raised this art to perfection. So the god Dionysus, apart from the gift of wine, gladdening the heart of man (and maddening him), allowing him to forget his daily cares, also bestowed on Greece one of the most important parts of its culture; the **theatre**.

Top right: Dionysus and Ariadne. Krater, 4th C. B.C. Centre: Dionysus and Semele. Etruscan mirror. Bottom right. Theatrical mask.

ASCLEPIUS

The son of Apollo and the Nymph Coronis, daughter of the King of the Thessalian Lapiths, Asclepius was born by the River **Trikkis** (today's Trikala). According to Pindar, however, he was born at **Epidavros**.

Apollo, the god of healing, wanted to hand this craft down to his son but not only did he succeed in this; his son surpassed him and became the god of medicine by studying with the **Centaur Cheiron**, a master in this art, how to treat every sickness and every wound, thus becoming famous and venerated throughout Greece.

One strange myth tells how Asclepius even learned how to resurrect the dead, using the blood of the Medusa given him by Athina. The perturbed Zeus, fearing that his power over mortals might be shaken by this act, struck Asclepius with lightning bolts, killing him. But, repenting, Zeus restored him to life and godhead and his descendents, the **Asclepiades**, among whom the most famous was **Hippocrates**, according to whose oath doctors around the world are sworn in, continued his work, developing medical science.

Other children Asclepius had with his wife **Ipioni** were **Podaleirius** and **Machaon**, who took part in the Trojan War as warrior-

Top right: Mosaic from Cos showing the arrival of Hippocrates on the island. Centre: Asclepius. Bottom left: The Temple of Apollo and the Asclepion on Cos, the most important in Ancient Greece.

Asclepius and Hygeia. Statue from Roman period. Vatican Museum.

doctors, and his five daughters, **Iaso**, **Akeso**, **Panakeia**, **Aigli** and the radiant **Hygieia** (health), each one of them with their own particular healing properties beneficial to mankind.

The first sanctuary of Asclepius (the **Asclepion**), was at Epidavros (beginning of the 5th C. B.C.) but there are nu-merous others throughout Greece: at Pergamon, in Attica and, chiefly, on the island of **Cos**.

Asclepia were various kinds of buildings dedicated to the god, like hospitals, attracting patients from all over Greece. Worshippers, once they had made a sacrifice to the god and taken part in **cleansing rituals**, so as to be psychologically and physically prepared, were admitted to a sacred place, the **Engoimitirio**, where the god appeared to them in dreams, showing them the best treatment to cure their minor ailments. In more serious cases the priests took part, following the guidance of the god.

After his death this great benefactor of mankind was set in the skies in the form of the constellation **Ophiouchou**.

The symbols of Asclepius were his **wand**, entwined with a snake and poison, which in small quantities can be curative.

His main site of worship, at **Epidavros**, in the Northern Pelopenossos, has one of the most perfect of all Greek theatres.

A large number of embossed reliefs representing different parts of the body, resembling the present-day "tamata", have been found at his temple as offerings to the god.

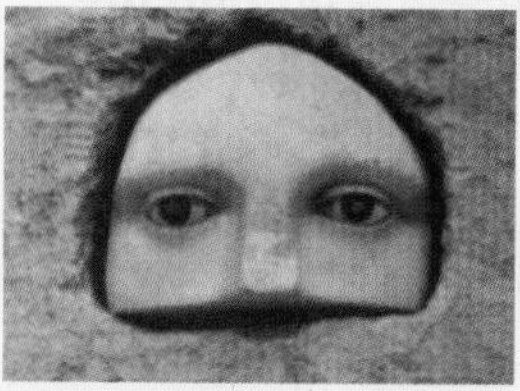

Above: An offering made at the Aesclapion of a pair of carefully detailed eyes.
New Museum of the Acropolis.

PAN

Pan might have been the son of Hermes and the nymph Callisto or, according to another version, Apollo and Oeneis. As a god he is closely identified with **fauna** and **flora** and nature in general, a personification of the generative life-force. He is a blend of human and animal features: a human body but with goats' legs and horns on his head (the **goat-footed god**), an erotic, playful, happy god.

He was born in **Arcadia**, on Mount Lykaio, and spent his life in forests and valleys and caves, by streams and cool springs, having erotic adventures and playing his shepherds' pipe. He was the protector of pastoralists and herders, adorer of wine and often to be found in Dionyssus's entourage.

From his numerous love affairs we will mention two of the most prominent.

Once he fell in love with the nymph **Syrinx** who, however, owing to his ugly appearance, did not reciprocate his love, pleading with the gods to turn her into a reed to escape his advances. And this was the very reed from which the god fashioned his **pan-pipes**.

Another story tells of his seduction of **Selene** (the moon) who, shining palely, crossed the night sky in her two-horse chariot. In order to have his way with her he

Top right: Aphrodite, Eros and Pan. Found on Delos. 2nd C. B.C.
Centre: Pan. Roman mosaic. National Museum, Rome.
Bottom: Pan chasing a shepherdess. Krater 470B.C.

transformed himself into an innocent sheep on which the unsuspecting Selene rode, with inevitable results.

The Greeks believed that he assisted them at the historic Battle of Marathon, appearing on the battlefield and crying out his name, over and over again, sending the Persians into a **panic**, a word derived from his name. For that reason he was particularly worshipped by the Athenians who dedicated caves (**Antra**) to him, throughout Attica, an important example of which is the one to be found in a cliff of the sacred rock of the Athenian Acropolis.

But his main place of worship was at his birthplace in **Arcadia**, where he was worshipped as a pastoral god, while the most ancient of his temples was to be found on Mount Lykaio, where the oldest group-games were held.

EROS

Illegitimate fruit of the union of **Ares** and **Aphrodite** Pandimou (that is; the goddess of fleshly pleasure), the ancients imagined him as a little naked boy with golden **wings** and a **bow** in his hand. Shooting **arrows** at the hearts of both man and gods, he awoke their passions and – according to Euripides – their unconquerable love, which can be distinguished as having both holy and negative elements, giving rise as it does, on the one hand, to everything good and pleasurable and, on the other, to the greatest suffering and ruin.

The god was beautiful, amusing, happy and playful, but his arrows were fiery and he was not to be toyed with, because as the son and instrument of Aphrodite, he punished

Top right Eros and Psyche. C.G. Cratzenstein-Stub, 1793 – 1860. Bottom right: Young woman and Eros. Bouguereau, 1676.

whoever failed to show them respect or neglected to honour them in the appropriate way.

Many portrayals of the god show him mounted on a dolphin or lion, symbols of his playful yet strong character. He also sometimes appears as a dazzlingly beautiful, athletic adolescent, the embodiment of youthful beauty, masculinity and sexual potency. The Romans referred to him as **Cupid**, fine pictures of which have been found at Pompeii.

Top: Eros and Psyche. Lionel Noel Royer, 1852 – 1926.

MINOR DEITIES AND OTHER MYTHICAL CHARACTERS

HELIOS

Helios, the sun, was represented as a god in early Greek mythology, probably the son of the Titan Hyperiona by his sister, Theia. Many believe that he can be identified with the god Apollo (the sun god), a theory that is untenable if you examine the relevant myths in detail.

He had two sisters: **Selene**, a beautiful shining goddess, personification of the moon, who crossed the night sky in her silver chariot, lending her pale but romantic light to the earth, and **Io**, the "*rosy-fingered*", as Homer calls her, goddess of the dawn.

Every morning he started out on his daily journey across the sky in the flaming **golden chariot** wrought by Hephaistus, from his magnificent Palace in Colchis in the east to the

*One well-known story is that of Helios's son, **Phaeton**, who pleaded with his father and was given permission to drive the **chariot of the sun** for a day. If he had stuck to Helios's instructions he might have managed, but , in the foolhardiness of youth, risked too much and lost control, sometimes flying low over the earth, drying the fields and rivers, especially in Africa, where he burnt the people black, sometimes high, in the frozen zones over the poles, so that everything froze. This crazy, uncontrolled ride was put to an end by Zeus who hurled a thunderbolt at the chariot to prevent it doing any worse, hurling Phaeton down into the River Eridanos, where he drowned.*

equally magnificent Palace in the Isles of the Blessed in the west.

The god Helios was worshipped in the Peloponnese, but the main centre was on **Rhodes**, where they held yearly games in his honour and, in addition built the huge bronze statue, the **Colossos**, one of the Seven Wonders of the Ancient World, in tribute to him.

Mention is made in the Odyssey to an island dedicated to Helios, grazed by his sacred red cattle: The **cattle of the sun**, some of which were slaughtered and eaten by Odysseus's men, thus incurring the anger of the god, destroying all of them save the hero himself, who had played no part in the act.

Helios is shown as a handsome youth, with a rich head of golden hair, crowned by sunbeams. He

Top: The god Helios driving the chariot of the Sun. Attic Krater of the Classical period. British Museum.

Centre: Fanciful reconstruction of the Colossus of Rhodes, one of the Seven Wonders of the World.

Top right: Muse holding a lyre. Lekane, the work of Asteas, 380 B.C.
Centre: Apollo and the Muse Calliope.Kylix 440 B.C.
Bottom: The Muse Melpomene carrying a theatrical mask, Achileo, Corfu.

had many children; apart from the unfortunate **Phaethon**, who rode too close to the sun, the sorceress **Circe**, **Pasiphae**, the wife of Minos, King of Crete, **Aiti**, king of Colpsida and **Medea**, also a sorceress.

Sol corresponds to Helios in Roman mythology.

THEMIS

The goddess of **justice**, protecting victims of injustice and punishing the unjust, daughter of Uranus and Rhea. Joining with Zeus she gave birth to the **Hours**, **Litigation**, **Just Government** (Evnomia), **Peace** and the three **Fates** (Lahesi, Clotho and Atropos) who govern the destiny of man, which can't be changed, even by the gods, from the moment of his birth.

Themis is usually portrayed blindfolded, carrying scales in her hand to weigh up mans' actions, because justice should be impartial, and is usually identified with law-trials.

THE MUSES

The nine daughters of Zeus and Mnemosyne, who dwelt on Mount **Helicon**, are followers of Apollo and protectresses of the Arts: **Clio** of history, **Calliope** poetry, **Euterpe** of lyric porty, **Thalia** comedy, **Melpomene** tragedy, **Polyhymnia** of sacred poetry, **Erato** of love poetry, **Terpsichore** of choral songs and the dance and **Urania** astronomy.

AEOLUS

The god of the **winds**, which he kept imprisoned in a bag, letting free only those he wanted to blow at the appropriate moment.

When, today, we say that someone opens **Aeolus's bag**, we mean that he's done something that will lead to

Top right: Oceanus and his sister and wife, Tithys. Roman mosaic.
Centre: Selene and Endymion. Wall-painting in Carlsberg, Copenhagen.
Bottom: Nereids.

disorder.

Aiolus and the winds are winged deities, as they appear on the **Tower of the Winds**, in Athens.

OCEANUS

The Titan son of Uranus and Gaia, the god of rivers, himself having the cyclical form of the river that surrounded the earth, the ancients believing that the earth was like a flat disc, with the dry land in the middle and Oceanus surrounding it. Together with his sister, **Tethys**, he had three thousand daughters, the beautiful Oceanides and three thousand sons, the **Rivers**.

THE NEREIDS

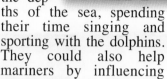

The fifty beautiful daughters of **Nereus**, an important sea deity and follower of Poseidon, lived in their father's palace in the depths of the sea, spending their time singing and sporting with the dolphins. They could also help mariners by influencing weather conditions

NAIADS

These are daughters of Zeus, mainly nymphs of springs, but also sweet water and lakes, giving water its healing power and love to mankind, many heroes, artists, poets and wise men being born as a result of their union with mortals.

NEMESIS

The goddess of **divine justice**, who punished those who transgressed the unwritten laws, the unjust and those who showed **hubris**, which can be defined as the over-estimation that

Top left: The goddess Eris on a cup, 6th C. B.C.
Centre: The goddess Chance on the shoulders of a swimmer. Roman copy of a colossal Greek original of the 4th C. B.C. Vatican Museum.

leads men to think that they can be better than the gods, the personification of this quality being, of course, the deity of the same name, Hubris.

There was a notable temple dedicated to Nemesis at **Ramnus**, in Attica.

HECATE

A great goddess, before the predominance of the twelve Olympians, daughter either of Perse (destruction) or of Zeus, who paid her especial honour, she was considered to be the protector of **magic** and is connected with the occult and the Underworld.

Her place of worship was usually at **crossroads**, considered to be magic places, where there were statues of her to which people made votive offerings.

NEED

The wise deity who the ancient tragic poets considered to be a supreme power, obeyed even by the gods. ("Need and the gods persuade").

ERIS

A loathed goddess who, wherever she happened to be, provoking dissention and strife. The failure of Pyleas and Thetida to invite her to their wedding brought disaster to them (see chapter "**The Apples of the Hesperides**"). Her daughter, **Atys**, followed in her mother's footsteps.

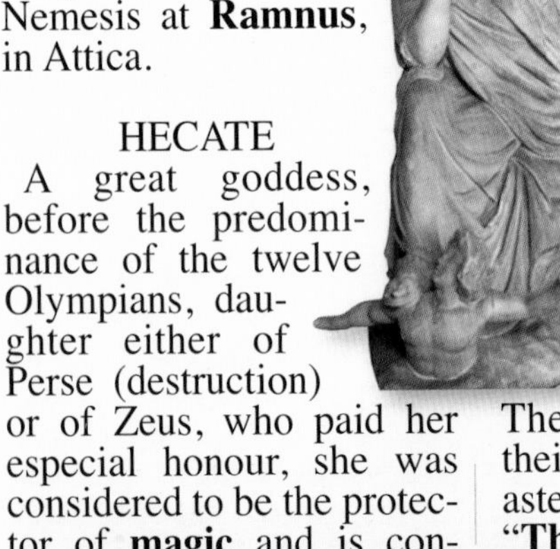

Cybele was an important and very ancient goddess, originating in the East, who was included in the Greek pantheon
Bottom left: Cybele giving protection against Vesuvius. Francois Eduard Picot, 1832.

Top left: The Sirens. H.J. Drapper.
Centre: Orpheus and Euridice. Michel Martin Drolling, 1789 – 1851.

ORPHEUS AND EURIDICE

Orpheus, from Thrace, son of the Muse **Calliope** and **Apollo** (his mortal father being King Oeagrus) was the most gifted musician and poet in Greek mythology. He took part in the Argonaut's expedition, but the myth for which he is most widely known is that of his great love for his wife, **Euridice**, a beautiful nymph who died after being bitten by a poisonous snake.

Wild with pain, Orpheus decided to go down into Hades to try to recover her. Playing his lyre he bewitched all who heard him, stopping what they were doing and forgetting their sufferings.

Pluto and **Persephone** were so moved both by the

OTHER DEITIES

A whole crowd of other gods who appeared in groups, such as the **Erinyes** (guilt), the **Kourites**, the **Gorgons** and the **Harpies**, as well as hundreds of minor divinities and demons, played their part in the inexhaustibly rich world of Greek mythology.

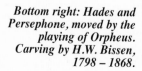

Bottom right: Hades and Persephone, moved by the playing of Orpheus. Carving by H.W. Bissen, 1798 – 1868.

heavenly music and by this manifestation of love that they offered to return Euridice, on the one condition that she followed her husband as he played his lyre, without once looking back, until they reached the upper world. Otherwise he would lose her forever.

Just before reaching the light, fearing that he was being cheated by the gods of the Underworld and unable to contain his uncertainty any longer, Orpheus turned and caught sight of Euridice's vanishing shadow. Turning back to Hades, he pleaded desperately for her return, but all in vain. Driven wild with grief, Orpheus never approached another woman.

The wonderful opera by Gluck, **Orpheas and Euridice**, tells this moving story.

After he had been torn apart by the **Maenads**, Orpheus's remains were collected together by the sorrowing Muses and buried at the foot of Mount Olympus. They say that he instructed the Thracian youth in the **Orphic life**, an austere, restrained style of living.

He is associated with rituals of the underworld (**The Orphic Mysteries**) which, some time in the 7th C. B.C. gave rise to a new religious movement, the **Orphic**.

Top right: Orpheus takes Eurydice out of the Underworld. Edmund Dulac, 1934. Bottom right: Women slaying Orpheus. Detail from an Athenian vase, 5th C. B. C.

ORACLES

Fear of the future and of disastrous events waiting to happen, is common to all mankind. For that reason people endeavour to find a way of foreseeing the future and in some way forestalling events.

In ancient times **oracles** were the main way of doing this and were of great importance, consulting them before making any important decision. When they had a problem and, generally, whenever they needed to communicate with the god to request his aid, they would send a representative or messenger to the oracle to ask for a prophecy. Such utterances were thought to express the will of the gods and therefore had to be obeyed by all people and, even, whole populations.

The most ancient oracle in Greece was that at **Dodona**, where both Zeus and Dioni were worshipped. Myth tells that two black doves were released from Egyptian Thebes. The first landed in Lybia, where they built the temple of Libyan Ammon, where there was an oracle, and the second flew to Dodona, where the sanctuary and oracle of Zeus were founded.

In the beginning it was an area open to the skies, centring on a **sacred oak tree** surrounded by **bronze tripods** which when clashed, together with the rustling leaves of the sacred tree and other natural sounds such as birdsong, streams and the wind enabled the priests to deliver the prophecy in words.

As time passed the oracle grew in importance and extent. A theatre, the oldest on Greek soil, was built, as were a parliament

Centre: Aegeus and the Delphic Oracle. Kylix, 5th C,B.C.
Bottom right: Apollo and the Python. Coloured sketch by Virgil Solis, 1514 – 1562.

building, a prytaneum, stoas and treasuries and Dodona grew to be the capital of **Epirus**.

The **Delphic Oracle** was the most important and famous of all, its influence extending far beyond Greece's borders. It was dedicated to the god of the oracular art, Apollo. According to tradition Zeus released two eagles, one of which flew east and one west, towards Delphi, which is reckoned to be the centre, the **navel of the Earth**.

The process of divination there was complicated: the **Pythia**, the **priestess** who delivered the oracle, after bathing in the **Castalian spring**, near to the sanctuary, seated herself on a tripod next to a rift in the earth; the place, it was said, where Apollo killed Python.

From this rift issued the smoke of burning laurel, the sacred plant of Apollo. Breathing in the smoke and chewing a laurel leaf, the Pythia went into an **ecstacy**, acting as a conduit between the god and the priests, uttering a kind of gibberish that had to be decoded by the priests and delivered as a prophecy that nearly always could be interpreted in two separate ways, often opposite to each other.

The oracle amassed much richness in offerings, nearly every town having its own small temple where its votive treasures were stored. Temples, theatres, hostels, a stadium, a whole town grew up around the Oracle. Every four years the **Pythia** were celebrated; Pan-Helladic games, including music contests.

Thus the Delphic Oracle developed into the greatest religious and cultural centre in Greece, constituting the **Pan-Hellenic Hestia** (hearth) and, for the first time in world history, international laws banning the execution of prisoners of war, the pollution of drinking water, etc were issued.

They say that the first priests of the oracle were **Cretan** and the first priestess to deliver Apollo's prophecy went by the name of **Sibyl**, a name that afterwards was given to various priestesses, the most famous being the Roman Sibyl who led Aeneus to the

Centre: The Pythia sitting over the chasm. John Collier.

Underworld.

There were also **Oracles of the dead** in ancient times where believers went to consult the souls of the dead, a bit like spiritualists do today. They were usually found in rocky places with caves and chasms, rivers or lakes, where, it was believed, it was easier for the spirits to reach light from the Underworld. The most important Oracle of the dead was at the River Acheron, deemed to be the entrance to the Underworld.

Other important oracles were those of **Didimaios Apollo** at Miletus, in **Lycia** and at **Thebes**. In all, in the 7th C. B.C. there were about a hundred of them in Greece. Later, with the development of more rational thought by Aristotle and other philosophers, oracles, in general, lost their authority, only that of Delphi maintaining its power, though hidden and weakened, right up to Christian times.

Apart from the oracles as establishments there were also famous individuals possessed with the power of divination: **Tiresias**, the blind prophet we meet in the myths of Oedipus and the House of the Lavdakidon, in Thebes, **Chalkas**, the main prophet of the Trojan expedition, many of whose prophecies came about, **Amphiaraos** and **Phineas**. Amongst the Trojans the most important were **Elenos**, **Lacoon** and **Cassandra**, who learnt the art from Apollo but, since she spurned his advances, was doomed by him only to forecast catastrophic events and never to be believed.

Oracles used different methods to predict the future, such as the flight of birds, the entrails of sacrificed animals and other natural **omens**.

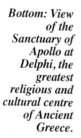

Bottom: View of the Sanctuary of Apollo at Delphi, the greatest religious and cultural centre of Ancient Greece.

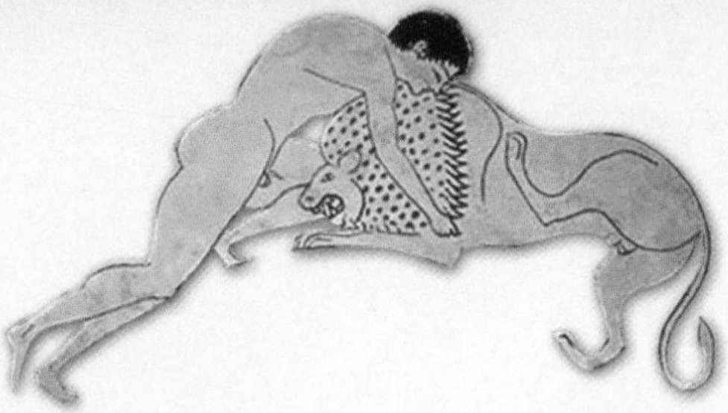

HEROES

HERACLES
THESEUS
JASON
PERSEUS
BELLEREPHON
MELEAGER

HERACLES

A very ancient mythical hero, the greatest in the ancient Greek world, a figure of extraordinary courage, generosity and strength, set down in the collective memory as the one who managed to accomplish the most daunting of feats.

His name is derived from the goddess Hera's name plus "kleos", which means "glory". That is: "Glory of Hera".

Even his birth was adventurous: his mother, **Alcmene**, daughter of the King of Mycenae and granddaughter of the hero Perseus, after fratricidal power-struggle, had taken refuge in Thebes, together with her husband, **Amphitryon**.

Blinded by her beauty, Zeus found his chance, once, when Amphitryon was away, to appear to Alcmene in the guise of her husband and have his way with her. Alcmene conceived Heracles. That same night, which was three times as long as a normal one, Amphitryon returned and also lay with his wife. So Alcmene was simultaneously pregnant with Heracles, from Zeus and **Iphicles** from Amphitryon. On the day of the births, Zeus boasted that the first boy to be born that day would be a ruler of men, King of the Argolid. Hearing this pronouncement, Hera became jealous and contrived to delay the births and hasten that of Nicippe, wife of the King of Argos, who forestalled them by giving birth to **Euristheus** who later Heracles served.

Hera didn't stop there; one day, while Heracles and his brother were asleep in the cradle, she sent a giant **snake** to kill them. But Heracles, displaying even in infancy his enormous muscular strength, grasped the snake and choked it to death.

Heracles was taught by **Lino**, Apollo's son, who

Top: Heracles by Glycon of Naples. 2nd C. B.C. Centre: The infant Hercules strangles the snakes sent by Hera. Attic stamnos, 480 B.C. Louvre, Paris.

taught him letters and music, but fell victim to his pupil's quick temper when, one day, he dared to criticize his performance and received in return a blow on the head with the lyre Hercules was playing, which killed him. Heracles wasn't punished, though, because **Rhadamanthus** had framed a law that put blame on the one who started the quarrel.

Once, when the youthful hero was standing at a crossroads, he was approached by two women. The first, called **Kakia** (evil), dressed in strikingly rich garments, told him that if he took the wide, easy way he would be happy and rich. The second woman, **Arete**, (virtue) promised him that if he followed the narrow, rough way he would be granted the praise, respect and love of gods and men. Without hesitation Heracles chose Arete's way.

Before he had even reached eighteen Heracles achieved a great feat, killing the **lion of Cithaeron**, and his fame began to spread throughout Greece.

Heracle's first wife was **Megara**, daughter of the King of Thebes, by whom he had

Another incident from Heracles's infanthood was when Hermes, at the command of Zeus, put Heracles to suck at **Hera's** breast while she slept, believing that the milk would endow him with godly qualities. When Hera became aware of what was happening – after the infant had had his share of milk – she angrily thrust him from her, the milk ("gala") that sprinkled from her breast becoming the **Galaxy**.

Top right: Hera suckles Heracles. Lekythos, 350 B.C. British Museum, London. Centre: Heracles at the crossroads. Pompeo Batoni, 1765. Bottom right: Heracles wrestling the lion of Kytheron. Kylix, 510 B.C.

three sons. There he lived happily, governing the city in the place of his father in law, who had abdicated the throne, until, once more, the vengeance of Hera struck. This time she sent Trela (madness) to unsettle his reasoning and the raging mad Heracles attacked and killed his wife and sons. **Athina**, his eternal protectress sped to his aid, knocking him unconscious with a stone. When he came to his senses and realized what he had done he wanted to put an end to his life, but the gods had other plans.

Consulting the oracle at Delphi, he was told that he must offer his service to the cousin of the King of Argos, Euristheus, and perform any labours that were given him if he wanted the blood-taint removed.

During the fifty days which Heracles was hunting the lion on Cithaeron, he was staying as a guest at the court of **Thespius**, King of the Thespians, who had fifty daughters. Wanting all of them to have children by this hero he sent a different one to sleep with him every night, which Heracles, not noticing in the dark, thought was the same one, only one of them refusing to take part in this ruse. In the end, though, there were fifty children, as calculated, one of them giving birth to twins.

The twelve labours of Heracles

Euristheus, out of a personal grudge, but also at Hera's instigation, exhausted every means he could to devise imposssible tasks, including encounters with supernatural beings, that would defeat or completely destroy the hero. These exploits, the most extreme that were ever achieved by a mortal, were known as the twelve labours of Heracles. Six of them were carried out in the Peloponnese and the other six in other parts of

Bottom: Heracles kills his children and destroys his home, watched by his terrified wife. Work of the painter Asteas, 4th C. B.C.

Heracles wrestling the Nemean lion. Francisco de Zurbaran, 1832. Prado, Madrid.

the then-known world.

Innumerable representations of them are to be found on vases, in sculptures, bas-reliefs and paintings, in Greek and world art.

The Nemean lion

The first of Heracles's labours was to exterminate the Nemean lion. This beast, that wrought terrible destruction, tearing apart human beings and animals, had been sent by the gods to punish the inhabitants of the area for neglecting their religious duties. It lived in a cave with two entrances and had a hide so tough it resisted iron.

On his way to Nemea Heracles cut a branch off a wild olive and fashioned it into the **club** which was ever after at his side. When he encountered the lion and saw that his arrows merely glanced off its hide, he forced it back into its cave, blocked the entrances, grappled with the beast and choked it to death. He wore the pelt of this beast, the **leonti**, all the time and, along with the club, it became one of his symbols.

In memory of this victory the **Nemean Games** were established, which, over the course of time, acquired pan-Hellenic importance.

The Lernaean Hydra

A mythical beast with a serpent's body and nine snaky heads, whose fiery breath could burn up anything that got close to it, the **Hydra** lived by Lake Lerna, feeding on herds. Heracles brought his beloved nephew **Iolaos**, the son of his brother, Iphicles, with him on this exploit.

While the hero tried to resist the monster, a huge crab, sent by Hera, harried him, snapping at his legs. From the stump of every head he managed to cut off another two sprung. So he told Iolaos to set fire to a nearby wood and fetch a flaming branch to burn the cut stumps to cauterize them and prevent any more heads from growing. With this means he destroyed

Top right: Hercules killing the Lernaian Hydra. John Singer Sergeant, 1856 – 1925.
Centre: Heracles, with the aid of Iolaus, cuts off the heads of the Hydra. Hydria, 6th C. B.C. Paul Getty Museum, California.

the Hydra, after having cut off the main, immortal head and burying it beneath a huge rock. Afterwards, Athina advised him to soak his arrowheads in the poisonous blood, making them invatiably fatal.

The Erymanthian Boar

On Mount **Erymanthus**, at the border between Arcadia and Elias, there lived a terrible wild boar who killed whoever he met in his path and generally wrought disaster. It was this animal that Euristheus commanded Heracles to bring back live and bound.

This was a difficult labour for him because he had first to exhaust the beast hunting him before he could be captured, bound and carried to Mycenae. When Euristheus beheld the boar he was so frightened that he ran and hid himself in a copper urn.

The Ceryneian Hind

The next task Euristheus assigned Herakles was to capture a deer with golden horns and brazen hooves, sacred to the goddess **Artemis**, and bring it back to him alive from Mount Ceryneia, in Arcadia, where it lived.

Legend said that Herakles pursued the hind for a whole year before finally managing to catch it. While he was carrying it on his shoulders back to the king he met Artemis who was enraged at this treatment given to an animal which was sacred to her. The hero explained that he intended it no harm, which reassured Artemis so much that she allowed him to take the hind to

Top right: Heracles bears the Erimanthean boar to the terrified Euristheias. Amphora. Classical period. British Museum, London.

Mycenae and show it to the king, on the understanding that afterwards he would set it free.

The Stymphalian Birds

On the shores of lake **Stymphalia**, in the mountains of Corinthia, amidst dense marsh growth, the carnivorous, man-eating, iron-plumaged Stymphalian birds had their nests and proliferated. Heracles's task was to get rid of them, which wasn't easy since they were deeply hidden in the dense, almost tropical vegetation.

But his constant help, **Athina**, came and gave him a pair of bronze rattles, made by Hephaestos, that made such a racket that it frightened the birds, flushing them out of the thickets outside which Heracles was waiting to shoot them with his poisoned arrows.

Thus he killed most of the birds, offering some to Athina in gratitude for her help, while those few that remained fled the country and took shelter on the Isle of Ares in the Black Sea.

The Stables of Augeias

King **Augeias**, son of the god Helios, kept huge herds of bulls and flocks of sheep in his stables in Elia, which he had neglected so much and for so long that the whole area was smothered in dung, not allowing plants to grow, polluting the water and the atmosphere and making life unbearable. Euristheus's order was that Heracles

Bottom left: Heracles shooting the Stymphalian Birds. Amphora, 530 B.C. British Museum, London.

should clear away all this filth in one day, with his bare hands.

During this humiliating mission, it occurred to Heracles that he might profit from it in some way. So he presented himself to Augeias and asked him to reward him if he cleansed the place. Not believing it possible that this could be done, Augeias agreed. After Heracles had dug some channels and conduits he diverted the flow of the rivers **Alpheius** and **Pineus** into them, sweeping the bulk of the dung into the sea, the remainder being scattered around the plain as fertilizer.

But when Augeias learnt that Heracles was acting under the instructions of Euristheus, he refused to pay him the agreed reward. So, later, Heracles and his allies waged war on Augeias and, after their inevitable victory, killed him, putting in his place his son, **Philea**, who became reconciled to Heracles when he realized the injustice his father had done him.

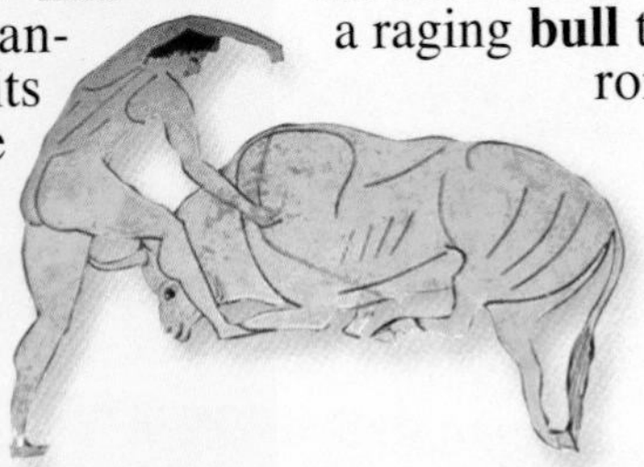

Centre: Heracles capturing the Cretan bull. Kylix, 515 B.C. The Tampa Museum, Florida.

In memory of this victory, Heracles decreed that contests should be held every four years at Olympia, in Elia, which developed into the famed **Olympic Games**, the most important in Greece and now around the world.

The Cretan Bull

The next of Heracles' labours was to capture live a raging **bull** that was terrorizing the inhabitants of Knossos, in Crete, and (wreaking havoc) there. It was possibly the same bull that **Poseidon** sent to **Minos** to show that he favoured him as king in preference to his brother (see chapter on the Myths of Crete).

Heracles, wrestling body to body with the bull, managed to catch him by the horns, tether and tame him, flying with him over the sea to Euristheus, who wanted to sacrifice him to Hera. She, however, unwilling to accept a gift that indirectly came from

Heracles, set the bull free.

After wandering through various parts of Greece, the bull reached Marathon, in Attica, where later the hero Theseus was to kill him. (see relevant chapter).

The Mares of Diomedes

Diomedes, son of the god Ares, king of the wild and warlike tribe of the Bistones in **Thrace**, had in his possession four terrible **mares**, the gift of his father, which fed on the flesh of whoever refused to obey him. Euristheus's next command was for Heracles to bring them to him.

This labour was difficult and required special preparation. After Heracles had armed and equipped a ship he requested assistance from various hero-friends of his, including Abderus and Locridus. When the boat reached the stables of Diomedes, who was, luckily, absent, they wiped out the guard and led the horses to the shore, where they were left under Abderus's protection. In the meanwhile Diomedes returned and, together with his tribe, started to fight against the invaders. The struggle between Heracles and Diomedes was long and hard but ended with a blow from Heracles' club.

Returning to the sea shore Heracles saw, to his horror, that the horses had torn his friend **Abderus** apart. After burying him in honour, Heracles founded a city in his memory, **Abdera**, where later the great philosopher **Democritus** was to be born.

Heracles appeased the rage of the mares by throwing Diomedes body to them, which, after they had torn it apart, succeeded in pacifying them enough that they could be conveyed to Euristheus, who sacrificed them to Hera, an offering she this time accepted.

Above*: *Heracles and Diomedes. Antoine Jean Gros, 1835.

Top right: Heracles' battle with the Amazons. Amphora, 520 B.C. Louvre, Paris.

Hippolyte's Girdle

The **Amazons**, who were probably daughters of **Ares**, were war-loving women who lived somewhere on the shores of the Black Sea. In their society the men played the role usually given to women, being used for reproduction and to carry out domestic duties. From their children they kept only the girls, who they brought up to be warriors, while they maimed the boys' arms and legs so that they were unable to fight.

ADMETUS AND ALCESTE

One beautiful myth worth mentioning here concerns Heracles's old friend, King ***Admetus****, who, when he stopped off to meet him in Pherrae, in Thessalia, found him deep in mourning for his wife,* ***Alceste****, because during their wedding, he had neglected to sacrifice to Artemis, and she, in retribution, had demanded his death – unless some relative of his would stand in his stead. His mother and father refusing to do this, Alceste offered herself in his place.*

Hearing this, Heracles decided to rescue Alceste from the Underworld. Waylaying ***Cheiron*** *before he went down to Hades, he fought with him and won, forcing him to return Alceste to her beloved Admetus.*

The tragedy by Euripedes and opera by Gluck both give moving accounts of this tale of faithfulness and love.

Top: *Wounded Amazon. Franz van Stuck, 1863 – 1928.*
Bottom: Hippolyta, the Queen of the Amazons, yields her girdle to Heracles.

The Amazons spent most of the time horse riding, fighting and hunting, cutting off one of their breasts in order to be able to handle their bows more easily. Their queen, Hippolyta, owned a golden gemstoned **girdle**, a gift from her father, Ares, and it was this that Euristheus' daughter desired and that the king commanded Heracles to bring to him.

Provisioning another boat he set out, with his companions, for the Black Sea, which he reached after a number of adventures. Recognizing him from his reputation, Hippolyte received him peacefully and, after he had explained the situation, offered to lend him the girdle. But Hera, who was always on the lookout for ways to harm Herakles, transformed herself into an Amazon and sowed division among him and Hippolyte, putting into her head the suspicion that his purpose was to overcome and destroy her. So the Amazons turned against their guests and fought them, Hippolyte was killed in battle and Heracles dispossessed her of the girdle.

The Cattle of Geryon

The tenth mission that Euristheus assigned to Heracles was to fetch him the wonderful red-haired cattle of **Geryon**, a monster with three joined bodies who dwelt in the west on the island of **Erytheia**. Along with Geryon the guardians of the cattle were **Eurytion**, son of Ares, and **Orthos**, Cerberus's brother, a terrible two-headed dog, with the tail of a snake.

Heracles was assisted on his journey by Hermes, who lent him the Horn of Plenty

to provide him with sustenance, as well as the golden goblet of the sun in which he crossed the ocean. On his way through Europe he came to the gulf dividing Europe from Africa in the Iberian Peninsula, today's Gibraltar, and as a memorial to his journey erected two columns, one on the African side, the other on the European; the famous "**Pillars of Hercules**."

When he finally reached Erytheia, he clubbed Eurytion and Orthos to death and dispatched Geryon with just one of his poisoned arrows, piercing him through all three of his bodies.

After many adventures, drawbacks and achievements which helped many people, Heracles returned to Mycenae with the cattle, which Euristheus sacrificed to his beloved goddess, Hera.

The Golden Apples of the Hesperides

An additional mission that was assigned to Heracles was to fetch Euristheus the **Apples of the Hesperides**. The trees that bore this golden fruit were to be found in Hera's **divine garden** on the slopes of Mount Atlas. They were the gift of mother Earth to Zeus and Hera at their wedding. When Hera found, one day, that Atlas's daughters, the three **Hesperides**, to whom she had entrusted the trees, had been stealing the apples, she set the hundred-headed serpent, **Ladon**, to keep watch over them.

Uncertain of his way on this long journey to the west of Lybia, Heracles consulted the oracular sea

Top left: Heracles attempts to slay with one arrow the three-bodied monster Gerion. Attic amphora, 550 B.C.
Centre: The Garden of the Hesperides. Frederick Lord Leighton, 1892.

deity **Nereus** who, however, reluctant to yield him any information, went through a series of transformations: into water, fire, then becoming invisible – the **metamorphoseis of Nereus** – Finally, though, Heracles caught him and forced him to show him the way.

During this adventurous voyage he had to fight the giant **Antaeus**, son of Gaia, which was very difficult because his strength was renewed each time he touched Mother Earth. Finally, though, Heracles managed to defeat him by raising him from the earth for long enough for his strength to ebb away completely.

It was also on this journey that he encountered **Prometheus**, shackled to a peak of the Caucasian Mountains, undergoing the terrible punishment of having his liver eaten every day by an eagle sent by Zeus (see chapter on Prometheus). Heracles killed the eagle, broke the bonds and liberated Prometheus who, in gratitude, advised him that the best person to help the hero on his mission was his brother, **Atlas**, who lived close to the divine garden, supporting on his shoulders the **dome of the sky**. He had to be careful, though, since the cunning Atlas might try to trap him.

And so it proved. When Heracles met Atlas and asked him for help, he himself offered to go and fetch the apples, asking the hero to carry the Heavens while he was away. With the aid of Athina, Heracles managed to shoulder the load while Atlas, assisted by the Hesperides, who

Centre: Heracles and Antaius. Hans Baldung, 1531.
Bottom left: Prometheus in the Caucasus. Rubens.

had managed to knock out **Ladon** with a sleeping potion, picked three of the apples. He thought, however, that a good chance had offered itself to rid himself of the task of bearing the heavens, a punishment visited on him by Zeus for fighting against him in the Battle of the Titans. (see relevant chapter on Atlas) leaving Heracles in his place.

The hero, however, practiced himself in trickery, asked Atlas to relieve him of the load just for a while, so that he could cushion the load he was not used to carrying. The moment he was free, Heracles went running off until he reached Euristhea and delivered the apples which the king gave as an offering to the goddess Athina who, considering their theft to be a great sin, restored them to the divine garden.

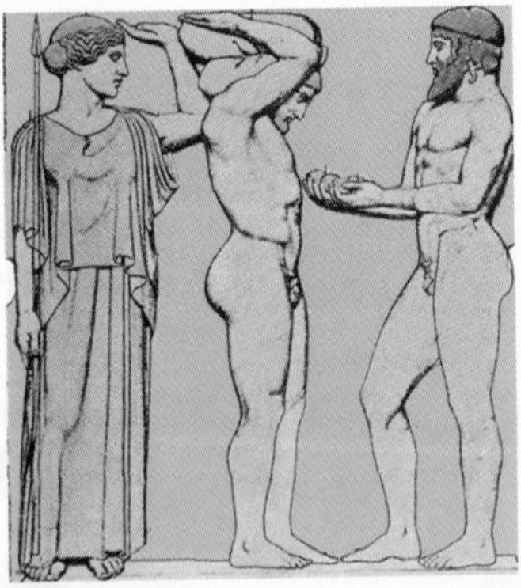

Cerberus and the Journey to the Underworld

Seeing that the time during which he had Heracles under his command was passing and that however difficult the task he set, the hero had managed to accomplish it, Euristheus decided to demand the impossible: that he go down into the Underworld and capture alive its guardian, **Cerberus**, a fifty-headed monster, the three in front in the shape of wild dog heads, the ones behind forming a tail of lethal serpents. This, the last of Hercules' labours, required him to transgress the natural laws which governed the sacred area of the Underworld.

Before Heracles undertook this insane mission, he underwent initiation into the **Chthonian Worship** at **Elevsis** – the cult of the Underworld. In addition Zeus commanded Hermes and Athina to accompany him in order to advise

Bottom left: Atlas offers the golden apples of the Hesperides to Hercules, while Athena waits to assist him. From the frieze of the Temple of Zeus at Olympia.

him in difficult situations.

Heracles, then, descended into Hades by way either of the gate at Cape **Taenaros** or from Lake Acheron. When he reached Hades, after having encountered the shapes of many famed characters from Greek mythology, he was presented to **Pluto** and **Persephone**, the rulers of the Underworld, and asked them for permission to take Cerberus with him for a while. Pluto conceded to this on the condition that Heracles should use no weapon in his capture. Wearing just his lion-skin, Heracles fought the monster and, after a terrible struggle, overthrew him, bound him and conveyed him to the terrified Euritheus, who took refuge in his favourite bronze urn. Heracles returned Cerberus to his place in Hades, as promised.

With that, Heracles accomplished the last of his Labours under Euritheu's command and was cleansed of the sin of murdering his wife and children.

Top left: Heracles, with the help of Hermes, brings Cerberus to Euristheia. Attic Kylix, 520 B.C. Centre: Heracles facing Cerberus. Francisco de Zurbaran, 1634.

Heracles' Downfall and Apotheosis

The greatest hero in Greek mythology achieved a lot more than his twelve famous labours. In the course of his turbulent life he even came into conflict with the gods, but, under the constant protection of Hermes and Athina, always came out on top.

He took part in the Battle of the Giants, on the side of his father, Zeus, journeyed with the Argonauts and on numerous occasions gave help where it was needed. He freed Promitheus from his chains and Theseus from imprisonment by the King of the Molossons in Epirus, saved Hesione,

Top left: Heracles kills Nessus, the centaur. Jules Delauney, 1828 – 1891. Centre: The same theme, from an Attic kylix, 420 A.D.

daughter of Laomedontas of Troy, from a sea monster and many other mortals in their hour of need.

The last and most fateful of his achievements was the killing of the Centaur, **Nessus**, who had attempted to abduct **Deianeira**, Heracles' second wife and sister of the hero **Meleager**, whose shade Heracles had met in the Underworld.

Up to then the couple had lived happily together and had had a son, **Hyllus**. On a journey together they had asked Nessus's help in crossing the river Evenus who, no sooner than he had Deianeira on his back, tried to abduct her, at which Heracles shot one of his poisoned arrows, killing him. Just before dying, Nessus revengefully told Deianeira to keep his blood and use it as a love potion with which she could triumph over every rival.

When, in due course, such a rival did appear, **Iole**, daughter of the King of Oechalia, and Deianeira learnt that Herakles was considering marrying her, she made a fine cloak for him and sprinkled it with

HERCULES AND OMPHALE

During Heracles's adventurous life he found himself once, as a punishment for stealing the sacred tripod of Delphi, serving as slave to ***Omphale****, the Queen of* ***Lydia*** *who, in order to humiliate him, forced him to dress as a woman and do household chores.*

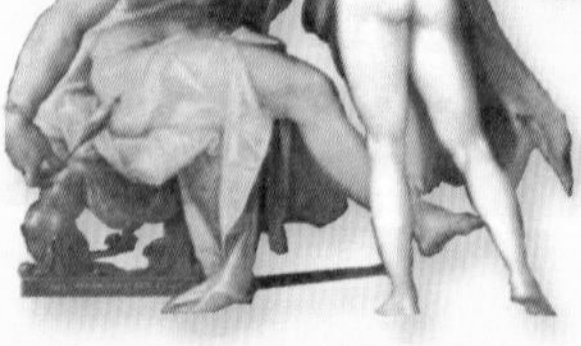

(Heracles and Omphalis, Bartolomaus Spranger, 1600.)

Top right: Heracles and Philoctetes. Ivan Akimovitch Akimov, 1754 – 1814.
Centre: Dianeira learns of Heracles' death. Evelyn Morgan.
Bottom right: Heracles' apotheosis. Francoise Lemoyne, 1736, Versailles.

Nessus's blood, not knowing that it was a strong poison, and sent it to her husband in Evoia in the hope that it would help him return to her.

When, however, the hero put it on, the poison started to burn his skin. And when he tried to take it off he pulled off his flesh. So agonizing was the pain that he became delirious and asked them to burn him to put him out of his agony, something that almost nobody wanted to do to such a great hero. Only **Philoctetes**, his son by Demonassa, pledged that he would build an enormous pyre on the peak of Mount Oeta – still today called "**Pyra**" - and Heracles, after giving his weapons to his son, lay down on it and was enfolded with fire.

But at that exact moment Zeus intervened, unleashing thunder and lightning from a great black cloud covering the area, under cover of which the goddess **Athena** conveyed Heracles to **Olympus**, where he was triumphantly received, reconciled with the goddess Hera, married **Hebe**, the goddess of youth, and took his rightful place among the immortals.

THESEUS

Theseus could be considered to be the answer of the elegant Ionians of Attica to the rough Dorian (Peloponnesian) hero Heracles, being only second to him in strength and reputation among the ancient Greeks.

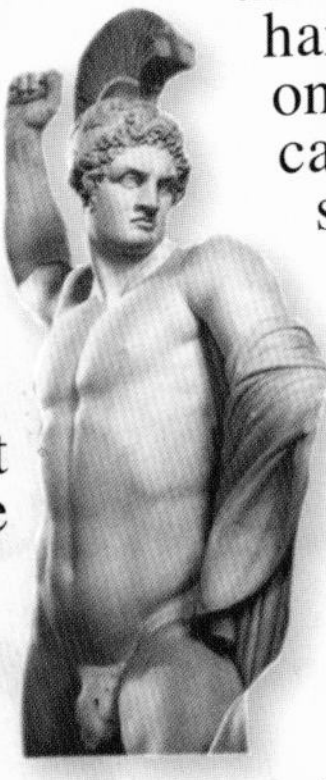

Aegeus, the King of Athens, although he had been twice married, was without issue and therefore decided to consult the Delphic oracle who delivered the strange prophesy that he should not untie the mouth of his wine skin until he reached the highest point of Athens, lest he should one day die of grief. This Aegeus could not interpret in any way.

On his way back he passed through **Troezen**, where his old friend **Pittheus** was king and he told him the prophecy. Pittheus, perceiving the meaning, after getting Aegeus drunk, contrived to have him sleep with his daughter, **Aethra**, with the intention of forging a tie with the royal family of Athens. When Aegeus recovered, he made Aethra promise that if a boy was born from their union he would be kept hidden, fearing that the Palantides, claimants to the Athenian throne, would try to harm him, and that only when the child came of age would she send him to join him in Athens. In order for Aegeus to recognize his son, he should bring with him the **sandals** and the **sword** that he hid under a huge rock.

Poseidon also slept with Aethra that same long night, so that Theseus's parentage is by no means certain. Very likely it was the god that succeeded, thus making the hero a demi-god, like Hercules.

Aethra did in fact give birth to a son, who she called **Theseus**, who gave evidence at an early age of his courage and strength. One day Heracles, dining

Top: Theseus. Statue by Antonio Canova, 1757 – 1822.
Bottom: Theseus raising the boulder underneath which is concealed his father's sword and sandals.

at Troezen with Pittheus, removed his lion skin and threw it over a stool. When the palace children came in, they screamed and fled, all except the seven-year old Theseus, who snatched up an axe and ran to attack the "lion".

When he reached the age of sixteen, Aethra, seeing how fearless and strong he was, told him the truth about his birth and parentage and, after he had raised the huge rock and found the sword and sandals, started out to meet his destiny in Athens. He was to achieve great things on this journey that would make him renowned throughout Greece.

The journey to Athens

At that time the land route from Troezen to Athens was plagued by thieves and ruffians who preyed off travelers. Theseus decided to take this route, and not the sea one, in order to get rid of these pests, both to earn praise for himself and to help others. The first of them he was to encounter was near Epidavros. It was the huge-bodied **Perephites**, son of Hephaestus, who killed passers-by with his club and robbed them. After a fight, Theseus managed to seize his club and batter the thief to death with it, afterwards keeping it for use on his exploits.

Top: Theseus and Sinys. Attic kylix, work of Elpinikos, 490 B.C. Munich. Centre: Theseus and Faia's wild boar.

Further on, at **Kechres**, one of the two ports on the Isthmus of Corinth, he encountered **Simis**, the "**Pityocamptes**" (pine-bender), so called because he would bend down two trees, tie the legs of his captives to them, then release them, tearing his victims in two. After a short fight Theseus ensured for his foe the same fate that he had afforded his victims.

Continuing on his journey he reached **Crommyum** where a terrible wild **sow** who guarded the crone, **Phaea**, was devastating the land. Here again the hero delivered the land and its people from this threat.

Following the coast road, Theseus came to the precipitous **cliffs** of **Sciron** (called Kakia Skala today). Sciron was a gigantic man who, after he had obliged travelers to bend and wash their feet, would kick them off the cliff into the sea, where a huge turtle was waiting to swallow them. When he tried to play the same trick on Theseus, he leapt aside and tumbled Sciron over the cliff. Killing the turtle, he made its shell into a shield.

Reaching **Elevsina** he killed the huge and powerful **Cercyon** who had forced wayfarers to wrestle with him to the death.

Finally, taking the Sacred Road to Athens, close to present-day Daphni, he was obliged to fight with **Procrustes**, a criminal who used a fiendishly ingenious means of torturing his victims.

Offering hospitality to travelers he would show them to their bed. If their legs were too long for it he would lop off their feet with an axe, while if they were too short he would stretch them on a kind of rack until they fitted, disjointing their limbs. Theseus, of course, turned the tables on him, cutting off not only his feet but his head to make him fit the bed.

Athens at last

When Theseus reached Athens his fame had gone before him, but even more adventures were awaiting him. In spite of the fact that he was traveling incognito, **Medea**, who after the death of her children had taken refuge in

Top: Theseus killing the Minotaur. Sculpture by Etiene Jules Ramey, 1796 1852. Centre: Theseus and the Minotaur. Roman mosaic Bottom: Theseus, carrying the clew, and Ariadne. 19th C. French artist.

Athens, guessed who he was and, because she feared that he would supersede her son, persuaded Aegeus, her husband, to assassinate him. The plan was to kill him with a poisoned drink at a banquet to which he would be invited. But when Theseus drew his sword to cut the meat, Aegeus recognized it on the instant, realized who he was and prevented him from drinking.

Enraged, Aegeus banished Medea and her son, **Medus**, who fled to Asia, to a country named **Medea**.

Theseus and the Minotaur

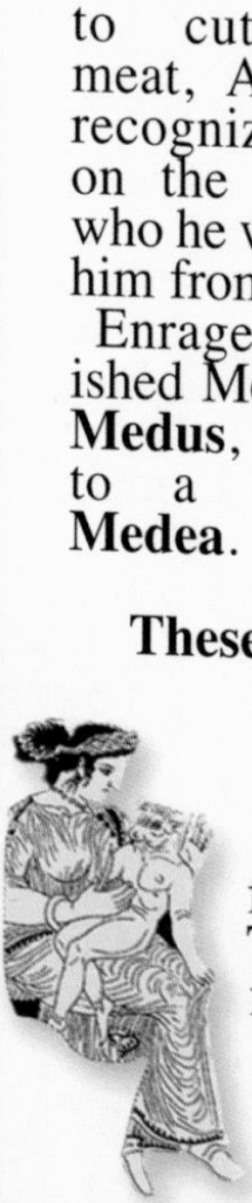

The greatest and most famous of Theseus's feats, it all began like this: After losing a lengthy war with Crete, Athens was obliged to sign a treaty, among whose terms was one that was especially harsh; Every year they had to send seven youths and seven maidens to Knossos to be sacrificed and fed to the **Minotaur**, a carnivorous, man-eating creature with a bull's head and the body of a man (see chapter on the Myths of Crete) who was kept closed up in the **Labyrinth**, a huge building designed by Daedalus (see chapter: Daedalus and Icarus) from which whoever entered found it impossible to escape.

When the time came round to pay this fearful

Top left: Thyseus killing the Minotaur, watched by Ariadne. Attic amphora 540 B.C. Louvre, Paris.
Bottom: Ariadne and Dionysus. Angelica Kauffman, 1741 – 1807.

tax, Theseus took the place of one of the youths, with the intention of killing the beast and relieving his city of this terrible weight.

The grieving Athina sent off the young people in a ship with black sails. Aegeus told his son that if his quest was successful he should change them for white, a sign that he was alive and well.

When the ship reached Crete, Theseus met King **Minos** and, after a dispute, proved that he was descended from Poseidon and thus entitled to enter the Labyrinth, which Minos, at length, agreed to, believing of course that he would never come out alive. Theseus had, however, already met the King's daughter, **Ariadne**, and been smitten with love for her and after he had made him promise that he would take her with him after the encounter with the Minotaur, she had given him the clew; a ball of thread that he would unroll as he walked through the maze and that would lead him out again. This is the well known ***"Ariadne's thread"***, a phrase we use today when we get our first hint of a solution.

And so it happened; Theseus found and killed the Minotaur after a long and terrible struggle. Rewinding the clew

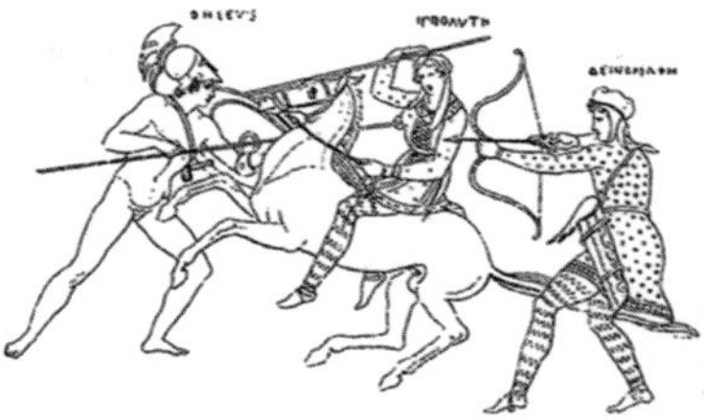

Top right: Theseus confronting Hippolytus and another Amazon. Centre: Theseus and Antiope.

he reached the entrance and found Ariadne waiting with the youths and maidens and the ship ready for departure. So they slipped silently and secretly away.

On their return journey they called in at **Naxos**, where Theseus had a dream in which Athina appeared and told him that, because Dionysos had fallen in love with Ariadne, he should leave her on the island. **Richard Strauss's** opera, "Ariadne in Naxos" tells of Ariadne's grief at her abandonment and of what happened thereafter.

On his approach to Athens, amidst all the excitement and anticipation, Theseus forgot to change his sails from black to white and Aegeus, who every day had anxiously searched the horizon from the cliffs at Sounion, seeing the black sails and thus believing his son to be dead, threw himself from the cliffs into the sea, which from then on was given his name: *The Aegean Sea*.

Theseus's reign, other feats and death

After the death of Aegeus, Theseus ascended the throne of Athens.

Skilful in government, he united the scattered settlements of Attica in a federation, with Athens, as their political centre. He also renamed the "**Athanaia**" celebrations in honour of the goddess Athina, the "**Panathanaia**" to symbolize the new political unity, making them even more impressive than before. He was an extremely philanthropic, popular ruler who made Athens into an important city, founding the first institutions of the Athenian state. He was also the first Athenian

Top right: Amazons attacking Athena. Relief by Adolf von Hildebrand, 1847 – 1921.) Centre: Theseus's Labours. Bottom: The death of Hippolytus, Rubens.

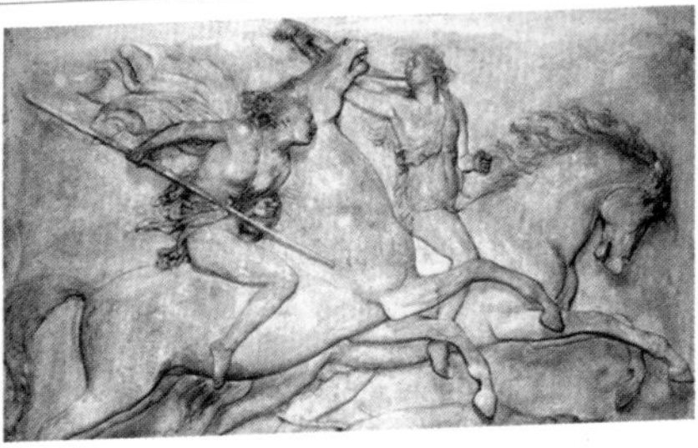

king to mint money.

During the course of his life he accomplished many achievements. He took part in the expedition of the Argonauts and accompanied Heracles on his quest to obtain Hippolyte's girdle (see relevant chapter on Heracles). There, he fell in love with the Amazon **Antiope**, brought her back to Athens, married her and had a son, **Hippolytus**.

Later, the Amazons launched an attack on Athens, in reprisal, but were defeated. During the struggle, however, Antiope was killed fighting at the side of her husband who mourned her deeply.

Another event in Theseus's life happened at the wedding of his childhood friend **Peirithous**,

*Years after the loss of Antiope, Theseus married **Phaedre**, daughter of Minos, with whom he had two sons. But this relationship was broken apart by Aphrodite in punishment for Phaedre's failure to sacrifice to her, causing her to fall in love with her stepson, **Hippolytus**. The innocent, worthy youth, however, rejected her advances and Phaedra, driven crazy by unappeased longing, killed herself, leaving behind a letter in which she accused him of making immoral proposals to her. Believing this, Theseus cursed his son and banished him. But as Hippolytus was leaving Athens his horses were startled by a beast invoked by his father, dragging him to his death.*

*This story is told in two great plays: Euripedes's "**Hippolytus**" and Racine's "**Phaedre**"*

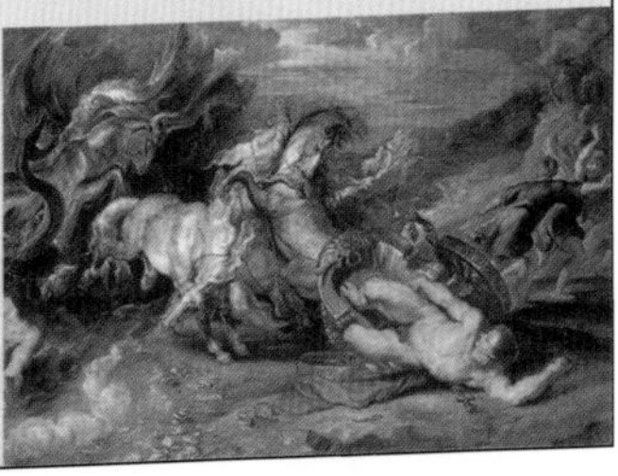

king of the Thessalian **Lapiths**. The **centaurs** who were present at the celebrations got riotously drunk and tried to abduct or even rape the Lapith women. Theseus and Peirithous resisted these terrible creatures, half horse, half man, killing many of them and driving the rest out of Thessaly. (See west pediment of Temple of Zeus at Olympia.

Unfortunately this great hero and wise king met an inglorious end. He was killed whilst on a voyage, on the island of **Skyros**, by King **Lycomedes** who, not wanting him to settle there, pushed him off the top of a high cliff.

In 475 BC the Athenian soldier, **Cymon**, transported the bones he was purported to have found on Skyros, to Athens where they put them in a monument to the hero they had built, the "**Theseon**" and proclaimed annual celebrations to his memory.

Top: Lapiths and centaurs. Antonio Canova.

When **Theseus** and **Peirithous** reached the age of fifty they decided to re-marry, vainly wanting their brides to be daughters of gods. So, after brazenly abducting **Helen** from Sparta for Theseus, they descended into Hades to steal **Persephone** for Pierithous. But **Pluto** fooled them both by getting them to sit on the **Throne of Lethe** (Forgetfulness) which, when they sat on it, became part of them, so that they were unable to get free of it. Theseus, however, had the good fortune to be freed by **Heracles** on his mission to the Underworld.

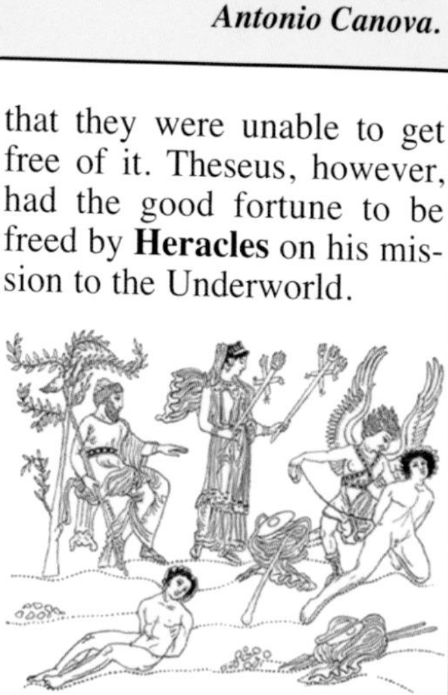

JASON AND THE ARGONAUTS

The **Argonaut** expedition was one of the most ancient and important undertaken in Greek mythology, many heroes known from other myths taking part in it. What were the events, then that led up to it?

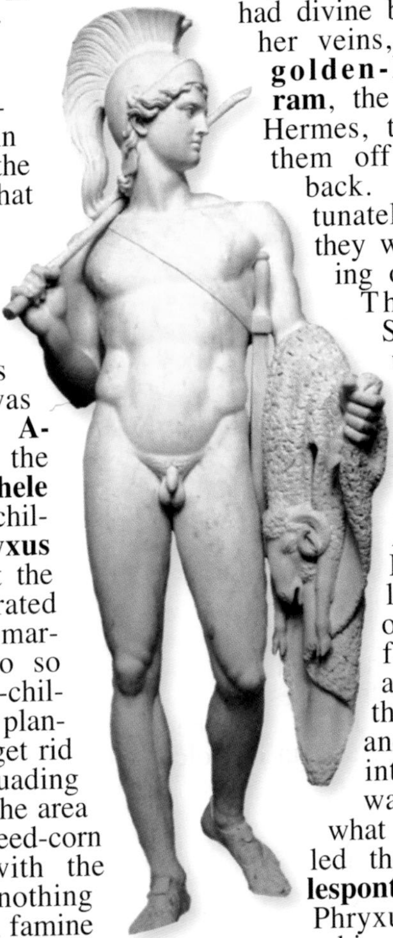

The Myth of Phryxus and Helle

Orchomenos in Boiotia was ruled over by **Athamus** and the Oceanida **Nephele** who had two children, **Phryyxus** and **Helle**. But the parents separated and Athamas married **Ino** who so hated her step-children that she planned a trick to get rid of them, persuading the women of the area to use their seed-corn for baking, with the result that nothing could be sown, famine falling on the land. Then she sent messengers to the **Oracle** at **Delphi**, bribing them to say that if they wanted the land to produce again they would have to sacrifice their children.

When, giving way to public pressure, Athamus conveyed his children to the altar, Nephele, who had divine blood in her veins, sent a **golden-haired ram**, the gift of Hermes, to carry them off on its back. Unfortunately, as they were flying over the Thracian Sea in the narrows between Europe and Asia, Helle leaned over too far, to admire the view, and fell into the waters of what then called the "**Hellespont**".

Phryxus continuing on his journey, reaching Colchis on the Black Sea, where he sacrificed the ram to Zeus and gave the **golden fleece** to **Aiti**, King of Colchis, who hung it on a sacred oak tree

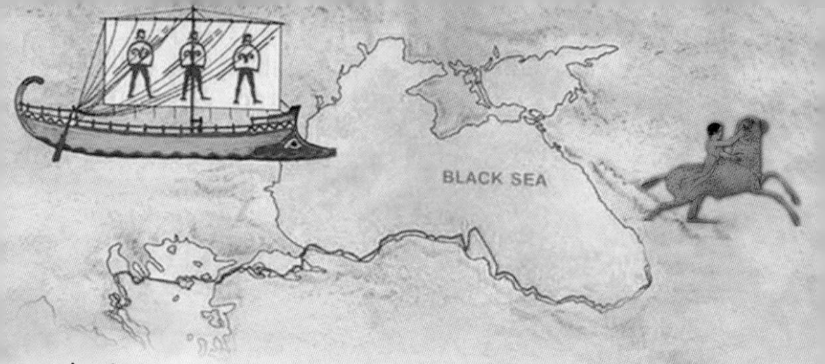

in the divine forest of Ares.

Jason

At that time the king of **Iolca** in Thessaly was **Pelius** who had usurped the throne in the place of the rightful heir, his brother **Aeson**.

Fearing for the safety of his son, Aeson spirited him away and delivered him to the care of the wise **Centaur Cheiron**, the most notable of the Centaurs, who taught him letters, arts and all the sciences of the times.

When Jason reached twenty he set out for Iolca to avenge his father's usurpation. On the way he met an old woman, Hera in disguise, who asked him to help her cross the river Anauros. Jason carried her over on his back, on the way losing one of his sandles.

Everyone in Iolcas admired the beautiful youth, only Pelius fearing him because a prophesy had told him to beware of someone wearing just **one sandle**. In response to Jason's claim be the rightful heir to the throne, Pelius, prevaricating, said that it would be delivered to him only if he gave him the **golden fleece**.

Jason, ambitious for glory, decided to go on this mission and started to pre-

Left: Jason and the Golden Fleece. Bertel Thorwaldsen , 1803, Copenhagen.
Centre: Phryxos escaping from Ino. Amphora, 440 B.C. Munich.
Bottom right: Phrixos and Medea sacrificing a ram.

Top right: The Argonauts.An oak branch from the sacred grove at Dodona is being nailed to the prow of the Argos. W. Russell Flint, 1880 – 1969.

pare for it, with the help of **Athina**. He engaged the famous craftsman Argo to build a large, light and seaworthy vessel, the **Argo**, to the prow of which Athina added a piece of wood from the sacred oak tree at Dodona, which was able to talk and predict the future.

The most famous heroes of the ancient world were invited to take part in the expedition and fifty of them accepted, among them **Heracles**, **Theseus**, **Meleager**, **Orpheus**, the **Dioscuri**, **Pelius** the **Myrmydon** and one woman, **Atalanta**, follower of Artemis, a swift runner and brave warrior. These were known as the **Argonauts**

Their first stop was on the island of **Lemnos** where they found that all the men had been murdered by their wives for their unfaithfulness and now there was no way that they could renew their race. So the Argonauts slept with them, creating a new generation.

They reached the **Symplegades**, two terrifying rocks that guarded the entrance to the Bosphoros, which, when a ship attempted to pass between them, clashed shut, crushing it. The seer **Phineus** who was with them, advised them to send a dove through in advance, which they did. As soon as the rocks had closed on her, nipping off a few feathers, and opened again, the Argo shot through at great speed, losing only a

Bottom right: Jason delivering the golden fleece to Pelius. Krater, 340 B.C. Louvre, Paris.

Top right: Athena assisting craftsmen to erect the mast of the Argo. Roman relief. 1st C. A.D.
Centre: Jason and Medea. Relief from a Roman sarcophagus. 2nd C. A.D.

part of the stern as the rocks clashed shut.

When they reached Colchis, close to the Caucasus mountains, they were presented to King **Aeetes** to whom they explained the purpose of their expedition. He agreed to give them the fleece, but only on two seemingly impossible conditions: Jason must yoke two fire-breathing, bronze-footed bulls and, with them, plough a field and sow in it dragon's teeth.

At this point **Medea**, Aeete's daughter, enters the story. Like her father, she was a child of the sun god, Helios and had learnt sorcery from her sister, **Circe**, becoming one of its most skilled practitioners. Smitten with love for Jason, Medea offered to help him, but on the understanding that he would take her away with him and marry her.

So she gave him a liquid that rendered him invulnerable so that he managed to yoke the bulls. But from the teeth he scattered sprung gigantic armed warriors. Following Medea's guidance Jason threw a rock in their midst and they, thinking it had been thrown by one of their number, began to fight among themselves so fiercely that not one of them was left alive.

Though Jason had fulfilled the conditions, King Aeetes had no intention of yielding him the fleece; it was only with Medea's help that he managed to

Bottom: The Argonauts confronting a dragon.

Top right: Medea preparing the magic potion to render Jason invincible. John William Waterhouse.

find it, guarded by a dragon, and to spirit it away in the Argo, with Aeete following in his ship in hot pursuit.

Medea then hit on a heartless ploy, killing her brother and throwing the dismembered corpse into the sea, so that her father would have to stop to pick them up. So, escaping, they crossed the sea to Iolca.

Jason and Medea

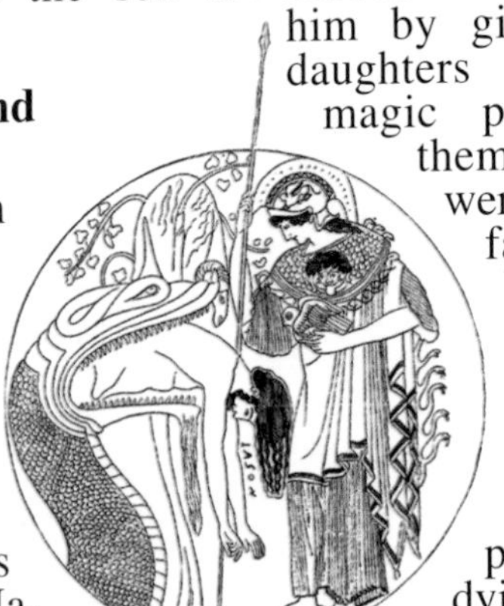

When Jason returned, however, Pelius refused to give up his throne, having already killed his brother – Jason's father – Aeson and all of his relatives. The one thing Jason wanted now was vengeance and, naturally, Medea was ready to help him by giving Peleus's daughters a supposed magic potion, telling them that if they were to kill their father, cut up his body, and boil it in that elixir, they would become young again.

So it happened, Pelius dying at the hands of his own children.

However, **Acastos**, Pelius's son, acting quickly, seized power. Jason, ex-

Centre: Athena rescuing Jason from the dragon's stomach. Work by Douris, 485 B.C. Vatican Museum.
Bottom right: Jason, helped by Athena, takes the Golden Fleece. Athenian vase, 470 B.C. Metropolitan Museum, New York.

Top left: Scene from the film: "Jason and the Argonauts.", 1963.

__Talos__ was the gigantic, bronze, guardian of Crete, a gift from __Hephaestus__ to __Minos__, whose duty it was to guard the island from unknown ships. Passing Crete on his way home, Jason with the help of Medea's magic, managed to kill the monster.

hausted by his efforts, left with Medea for Corinth, where they lived happily together for ten years until Jason fell in love with **Glauce**, daughter of the Corinthian king, and decided to separate from Medea and remarry.

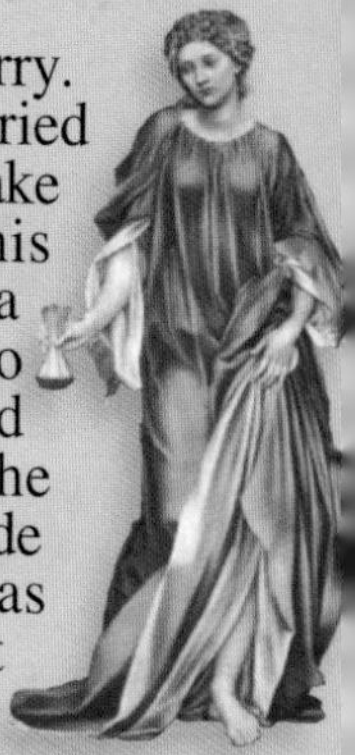

After having tried every way to make Jason change his mind, Medea resorted again to witchcraft and murder. First she sent Glauce a bride dress which, as soon as she put it on, burst into flame, burning not only she herself alive, but her father as well in his efforts to save her. Then she committed an act so disgusting and ignoble that it made her name infamous through history, killing her two children with her own hands. The story of Medea's bloody revenge is told in **Euripides**' play of the same name.

After these murders Medea fled from Corinth and found refuge in Athens with King Aegeus, by whom she had a son, Medeius.

In an attempt to get over his suffering, Jason wandered from city to city, hated of men, meeting an ignoble end in Corinth, killed by chance next to his old boat, the Argo.

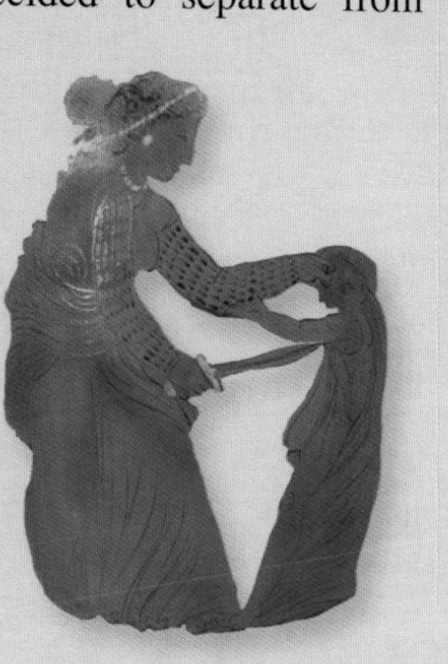

Top right: Medea. Detail from a painting by Evelyn Pickering de Morgan.
Bottom left: Medea stabbing one of her children. Amphora, 3rd C. B.C. Louvre, Paris.

PERSEUS

Acrisias, King of Argos, had a beautiful daughter, **Danae**, but a prophesy had told him that the son of his daughter would kill him. Not wanting her to come into contact with any man he kept her shut up in a dungeon. **Zeus**, however, who had already become enamoured of her, transformed into a **golden shower**, penetrated both the prison and the lady. From that union came **Perseus**, a secret Danae managed for to keep hidden from her father a while.

But when Acrisias learnt of the child's existence he had his daughter and the infant Perseus put into a box and set adrift on the sea, hoping that they would drown, but instead the current carried them to the island of **Seriphos**, where they were found by a fisherman, *Dictys*, who took them under his protection, rearing Perseus as his own child.

However, the King of Seriphos, Polydectes, fell in love with Danae and wanted to marry her, against her will. To get rid of Perseus, who stood in his way, he set a trap; he invited him to a banquet, knowing that the young man had nothing to offer him by way of a gift, demanded that he bring him the head of the **Gorgon Medusa**, threatening that if he failed to do this, he, Polydectes, would force Danae into marriage.

Top right: Zeus, in the form of a golden shower, fertilizes Danae. Krater from Boiotia, 450 B.C. Louvre, Paris.
Centre: Perseus with the head of Medusa. Benvenuto Cellini. Florence.
Bottom: Danae and the golden shower. Titian.

Perseus, Medusa and Andromeda

The Medusa **Gorgo** was one of the three Gorgons, sea monsters with snaky hair and such a frightening appearance that whoever looked on them was turned to stone. She was the only one of the three who was mortal.

Both **Hermes** and **Athina**, the protectors of heroes, helped Perseus through this difficult trial, giving him Pluto's **hood** of invisibility, a magic sack and **winged sandals** for use on his mission.

Flying with the winged sandals over the sea coasts, Perseus came across the Gorgon asleep. Following Athena's advice he didn't look at the monster directly, but at her reflection in his highly polished shield and, with the sword that Hermes had given him, cut off the **Gorgon's head** and put it into the magic sack. From the severed neck of the Medusa sprang the winged horse, **Pegasus**.

Managing to escape the other Gorgons who pursued him, he reached the land of the **Ethiopians** and saw before him a beautiful young woman chained to a rock, left there to be eaten by a sea monster as a sacrifice to Poseidon, who had sent famine to the country. This

Top right: Perseus, mounted on Pegasus, rescues Andromeda. Guiseppe Cesari, 1568 – 1640. Bottom right: Perseus giving the head of Medusa to Athina.

was **Andromeda**, the King's daughter. After Perseus killed the monster and set Andromeda free, her parents were glad to give the hero her hand in marriage.

Returning with Andromeda to Seriphos he found that Polydectes had threatened Danae and Dictys so much they had taken refuge in a temple. Going straight to the palace where Polydectes and his companions were banqueting he took the head of the Gorgon out of the magic sack, turned both him and his company to stone. He then raised Dictys to the throne of Seriphos and left with Andromeda in search of his grandfather.

But destiny pursued him: throwing the discus at an athletics competition, he accidentally hit his grandfather, **Acrisia**, who happened to be there in the crowd, killing him. When he learnt who it was, he had him buried with great honour and then, being ashamed to rule in Argos, made an agreement with **Megapenthis**, King of Tiryns, to swap kingdoms.

Through wise administration, Perseus managed to extend the Argolid state, building golden **Mycenae**, one of the most important cities of prehistoric Greece.

***Centre**: The head of the gorgon, as it appeared on Athena's shield.*

*Perseus dedicated **Medusa's head** to **Athena**, who had it set at the centre of her shield – the famous "**Gorgoneio**" which still in death had the power to turn all who looked on it to stone.*

BELLEROPHON AND PEGASUS

The myth of Bellerophon is one of the most poetic and widespread in Greek mythology. Let's continue the story from the last chapter, where we related that Pegasus sprung from the neck of the beheaded Gorgon.

This wonderful winged horse was given by Poseidon to his son **Bellerophon** who lived in Corinth and had **Glaukus**, the son of Sysiphus, as his mortal father.

Bellerophon unintentionally killed someone and

***Sisyphus**, the son of the wind-god, Aeolus, and founder of Corinth, though mortal managed to return twice from the Underworld, cheating the gods and overthrowinging the natural order. When, however, Hermes led him down a third time, the judges of Hades condemned him to push up a hill a great round boulder which, whenever he neared its crest, rolled down again, obliging him to begin his perpetual effort over and over again, the so-called **torture of Sisyphus**.*

was obliged to leave his homeland and take refuge at the court of his friend, **Proetus**, King of Tiryns, who purified him of the his sin and offered him hospitality. Proetus's wife, however, fell in love with the handsome young stranger, who would have nothing to do with her advances. So, in retribution, she told her husband that Bellerophon had tried to rape her. Being unable himself to take action, because of the laws of hospitality, which were sacred, he sent the young man to his father-in-law, **Iobates**, King of Lycia, with a sealed letter containing instructions to kill the bearer.

The letter, however, slipped Bellerophon's memory for nine days, allowing him to enjoy all the honours and pleasures afforded to guests by Xenios Dias, the god of hospitality. When, on the tenth day, he presented the letter to Iobates who, finding hiself facing the difficult situation of not being able to violate the sacred law, thought of another way of disposing with his guest, by asking him to do an unachievable task; to kill

Top left: The Torture of Sisyphus.. Detail of a painting by Titian, 1549.
Bottom right: Bellerophon and Pegasus. Carving by Julius Troschel, 1850. New Gallery, Munich.

Top right: Bellerophon and Pegasus. Alexander Ivanov, 1806 – 1858.

the **Chimera**, a terrifying monster with three fire-breathing heads – goat, lion and dragon.

His father, Poseidon, sped to his aid, bringing Pegasus with him to give to his son, the horse being so wild that he could only be governed by the golden reins brought by Athina. Flying high over the Chimera, Bellerophon let loose a shower of arrows and killed the beast.

After this trial, Iobates sent Bellerophon on many missions against wild tribes such as the **Amazons** and, since he always returned triumphant, the king bowed before the courage of the hero, acknowledged his godly descent and granted him both half his kingdom and his daughter into the bargain.

Unfortunately, though, all this praise at his achievements went to Bellerophon's head, even daring to aspire to fly Pegasus up to Olympus. But when Zeus heard of this, he determined to put an end to this **hubris**, commanding Pegasus to throw him down to the earth. So the hero, lame, half out of his wits, cast out by god and man, dragged out the rest of his life, alone.

Bottom right: Meleager, the Caledonian Boar and a hunting dog. Roman copy from 150 A.D. of an older Greek original. Vatican Museum.

MELEAGER AND THE CALIDONIAN BOAR

Once **Oeneus**, the King of **Calidonia**, left Artemis out of his offerings and, in retribution the goddess sent a fearsome boar to ravage the area. Oeneus's son, Meleager, who had made friends with many heroes on the Argonaut expedition, asked for their aid to hunt down the animal. He was also helped by **Plevron**, chief of the **Curitis** and the beautiful and swift female warrior, **Atalanta**.

After a long and exhausting chase, during which Plevron managed to wound the boar, Meleager finally succeeded in killing it. Rivalry had arisen between the hunters as to who should take the pelt of the animal, leading to a fight between those from Callidon and the Curitis, leading, amongst other fateful things, to the death of Meleager.

Top right: Meleager and Atalanta. Gerrit von Hornthorst, 1590 – 1656.
Centre: The Chimera. Plate, 350 B.C. Louvre, Paris.

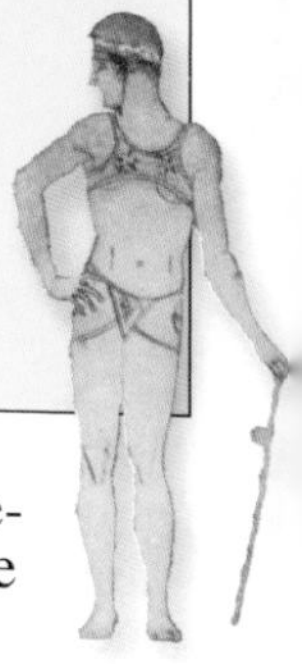

Bottom: The hunt for the Calydonian Boar. Peter Paul Rubens, 1620.

MYTHICAL CYCLES

ATTIC MYTHS

Athens was first named **Aktiki**, after the name of its first king, **Actaeon**. This was then changed to Cecropia, derived from another of its kings, Cecrops, a mythical being with the body of a man and the tail of a serpent. He had three daughters: **Pandrosos**, **Herse** and **Aglauros**

During his kingship there was rivalry between Athina and Poseidon for the guardianship of the city to which they both offered gifts. Poseidon drew forth a spring of sea water and a beautiful horse, smiting the rock of the rock of the Acropolis with his trident, while Athina offered an olive tree. The citizens, under Cecrops, decided in favour of Athina's gift, because it symbolized peace and prosperity. So they dedicated the city to her and gave it her name, paying her special honour in the celebration of the **Panathinaia** and building on the rock of the Acropolis the most important temple in the ancient world, the **Parthenon**.

Cecrops, a prudent king framed laws, established the institutions of marriage and burial and organized the independent townships of Attica into a federation, thus creating the **Athenian state**. One of his descendents, **Atthis**, gave his name to the women of Athina, who were called **Atthides**, but also to the whole area, **Attica**. Among the most important of the kings of Athens were **Erechtheius**, **Aegeas** and **Thyseus**.

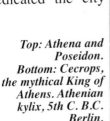

Top: Athena and Poseidon. Bottom: Cecrops, the mythical King of Athens. Athenian kylix, 5th C. B.C. Berlin.

Codros, disguised as a countryman, offers himself to be sacrificed to save Athens. Domenico Beccafumi, 1535.

The last king of Athens was a descendent of Ellina, **Codros***, who ruled somewhere around 1,000 B.C. One of the most moving of the Attic myths is associated with him.*

The **Dorians** *of the Peloponnese invaded Attica on account of the great drought ravaging their land which hadn't affected Attica at all. Before gathering their forces, though, they had consulted the Dephic Oracle and been told that in order to be victorious they must avoid killing the king of Athens. But someone told this to the Athenians and Codros decided to sacrifice himself in order to save the city. Dressed as a countryman he approached the enemy camp. There he stirred up an argument with two soldiers and, after he had killed one, insulted the other so badly that he killed him.*

The Athenians sent a messenger to the camp to ask for the body of their king. When the Dorians understood what had happened they withdrew from Attica.

After the Athenians had buried their king on the **sacred rock** *of the* **Acropolis** *the Athenians decided to make his name remembered by vowing never to have a king again. Codros's tomb was, according to witnesses, still to be seen on the eastern slopes of the Acropolis up to the 2nd C. A.D.*

The story is an account, in mythical form, of the abolishment of kingship and, in general, of the origin of those democratic institutions that were to make Athens the most brilliant Greek city and the greatest naval power of its time.

CRETAN MYTHS

Crete, after whom the island was named, was one of the Hesperides, a daughter of **Asterius**. She was the first wife of King **Minos** and mother of his second wife, **Pasiphae**, through her union with the sun god, Helios, while with Zeus she had a daughter, Cara. Another version attributes the name of the island to **Kris** (father unknown) a son of the nymph Idaia, a native of Crete and its first law-giver.

The Cretans were keen seafarers and, under King Minos, became the greatest naval power in the Mediterranean, their civilization reaching its acme.

It was on Crete that **Zeus** was born and where he came with **Europe** after abducting her. After he had married her to the king of the island, Asterius, so that his offspring would have rights to the throne of Crete, she gave birth to three sons: **Minos**, **Rhadamanthus** and **Sarpedon**.

After Asterius's death his sons fell into disagreement over the succession and Minos sought for some heavenly sign to show that he was the one favoured by the gods. Thus it was that Poseidon sent a wonderful **white bull** from the sea, ordering that it should be sacrificed to him. But Minos, bewitched by its beauty, tried substituting another animal in the hope that the god wouldn't notice. The punishment wasn't late in coming; Poseidon, with the aid of Aphrodite, smote Pasiphae, his wife, with a strange erotic yearning for the beautiful white bull.

So great was her longing that she asked Daedalus to construct for her a hollow wooden model of a cow, covered in skin, into which she would climb to be mounted by the bull. The result of this successful subterfuge was the creature she gave birth to; half man, half

bull; the renowned, bloodthirsty **Minotaur**.

Minos commissioned Daedalus to construct a fiendishly complex building, the **Labyrinth**, in which he imprisoned the monster. On Crete the bull was worshipped and the greatest celebration on the island was the **Tavrokathapsia**, dedicated to Poseidon

Under King Minos, as we have said, Crete became the greatest sea-power of the Mediterranean, developing trade and the arts during a period of peace and prosperity. The magnificent palaces of **Knossos** and **Phaistos** show the heights this culture reached.

This most famous King of Crete was also a great law-giver. It is said that every nine years he went up to the **Idaion Andron**, the cave on Mount Ida (Psiloritis) where Zeus was said to have been born, and, in collaboration with the god, framed his just laws.

Centre: The Minotaur. Attic kylix, 515 B.C. Madrid.
Bottom: The bull-leaping ceremony and celebration. Wall painting from Knossos. Archaeological Museum, Heraclion.

Minos had many children with Parsiphae: **Acacallis**, **Ariadne**, **Androgeus**, **Catreus**, **Glaucus** and **Phaedra**. Minos was succeeded by Catreus. Minos is said to have ruled for many generations, together with his bother **Rhadamanthus**, whose name became synonymous with good judgment and who wielded power so justly that his state became the most important of its time.

After their deaths they became the two eternal

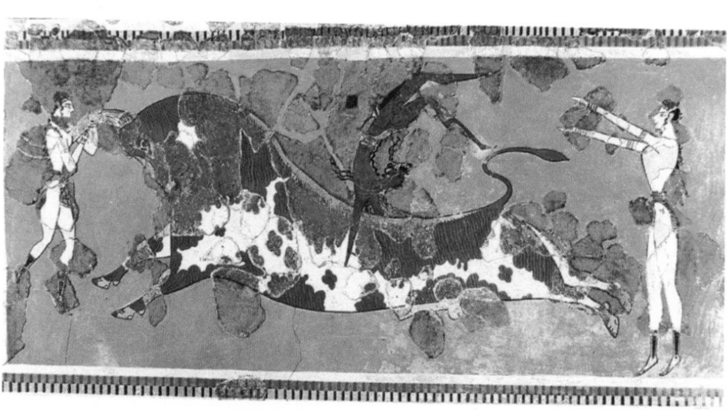

Right: "Take care". The final, disregarded, advice Daedalus gave his son, Icarus. From a painting by Antony van Dyck (1620).

judges of the dead in Hades. Their other brother, **Sarpedon**, went to Asia Minor where he became the King of **Lycia**. He lived for three generations, founded **Miletus** and was worshipped as a god.

One of Minos's nephews, **Kydon**, son of Akakalida and Hermes, built the city of **Kydonia** – the present-day Chania – in Western Crete, while another of his descendents, **Idomeneas**, son of Levkalion, was especially noted for his bravery in the Trojan War.

> Once, **Androgeus**, the son of Minos, went to Athens to take part in the **Pan-Athinaic Games** and was victor in every event he entered, provoking the envy of the Athenians, who sent him to kill the bull of Crete, at that time ravaging Marathon. The young man was killed in the attempt and his father, **Minos**, led a force against the Athenians which defeated them and, in reprisal for the death of his son, he imposed a **blood tax** of seven youths and seven maidens to be given to the Minotaur (see chapter on Theseus).

Daedalus and Icarus

Athenian in descent, from an ancient royal line, **Daedalus** was looked upon as being the greatest inventor, architect, sculptor and, in general, the most skilled in the science of art, a pioneering spirit who is credited with inventing the drill, the saw, the potter's wheel, the plumb line, among other things.

His assistant in his workshop in Athens was his nephew **Talos**, an extremely skilled technician who also claimed to have invented the saw, as well as the compass. Daedalus, fearing that Talus's reputation would surpass his own, killed him by pushing him off the Acropolis, for which crime he was sentenced, by the High Court, to banishment.

So it was he came to

Top right: Daedalus and Icarus. From a painting by Frederick Leighton, 1830 – 1896.
Bottom right: The fallen Icarus. Herbert James Draper, 1860 – 1920

Crete, where he was hired by King Minos to plan and build the royal **palaces** at Knossos and Phaestos. In addition he built the **Labyrinth**, a maze-like construction built so that whoever entered it would never emerge again.

He married **Naucrate** with whom he had one child, **Icarus**.

Minos, however, grew dissatisfied with him, one reason being that he had helped his wife, Pasiphae to mate with the bull, and another that he had given **Ariadne** the clew that Theseus had used to seek out the Minotaur and to escape (see relevant myths). He also didn't want to allow him to offer his services to anyone else. And so he banned him from leaving the island.

In response to this, Daedalus's inventiveness went into overdrive; he fashioned huge wings, some of the feathers of which were stuck together with wax and, after fastening them onto himself and his son, warned him to fly neither too high nor too low but to follow him closely.

So they set out on their great attempt, the first of all mortal flights. But the young man, in the foolhardiness of youth, flew too near the sun, which melted the wax that held his feathers together and he plummeted into the sea, which ever after took his name, the "**Icarian Sea**."

THE MYTHS OF THEBES CADMUS AND THE HOUSE OF LABDACUS

Cadmus, brother of **Europe**, was so ashamed that he didn't manage to bring her back after her abduction by Zeus that he couldn't return to his homeland. Instead, he went to Delphi to ask the Oracle where she could be found and was told that he should give up the search and follow a cow and wherever the cow lay down found a city.

The cow stopped in a fertile valley in Boiotia and there Cadmus built the city of **Thebes**, whose Acropolis was called the **Cadmia**.

He married **Harmony**, the daughter of Ares and Aphrodite and is said to have taught the Greeks the **Phoenician alphabet**.

His grandson **Labdacus** gave his name to his whole lineage, the **Labdacides** which had such a terrible fate that, together with the house of Atreus, they are the chief source of inspiration for the great tragic poets.

Centre: Cadmus and Harmony. Evelyn Pickering de Morgan, 1877.
Bottom right: Cadmus and the dragon. Kalyx, work of Python, 350 B.C.

Oedipus

The story began when **Laius**, after succeeding Labdacus to the throne of **Thebes**, married **Iocasta**, the sister of **Creon**. Since the marriage was unfruitful, he addressed the Delphic Oracle and was delivered the bleak prediction that Iocasta's barrenness was a blessing in disguise since if she were to bear a son he would kill his father, with catastrophic consequences

for all. So when in the fullness of time Iocasta did become pregnant and give birth to a son, he commanded a servant, in panic, to take the child and leave it exposed on **Mount Cithaeron**, to be eaten by wild animals, binding the child's ankles with thick chains.

The servant, however, took pity on the child and gave it to a shepherd who took it to his home in **Corinth** and offered it to the childless royal couple, **Polybus** and **Merope**, who reared him as their own, giving him the name of **Oedipus**, on account of his swollen feet.

When Oedipus had grown up and was ready to succeed Polybus, who he regarded as his father, to the throne of Corinth, somebody dropped a remark questioning his origin and legitimacy. After questioning his supposed parents and receiving no answer he appealed to the Delphic Oracle and was delivered the terrible prediction that he would kill his father and marry his mother.

Top right: Oedipus and the Sphynx. Detail from a painting by Gustave Moreau, 1826 – 1898. Metropolitan Museum, New York. Centre: Oedipus and the Sphynx. Attic kylix. Vatican, Rome.

Deeply shaken, still believeing his parents to be Polybus and Merope, he avoided returning to Corinth and wandered the roads, quite by chance encountering Laius, his true father, in his chariot, without, of course, knowing who he was.

When Laius imperiously ordered him out of the way he stood his ground. A quarrel started during which Laius struck him and, in retaliation, Oedipus killed him, thus fulfilling the first part of the oracle's prediction.

At that time a creature called the **Sphinx**, which had the body of a lion, a woman's head and wings,

had taken control of a pass,
vhere she demanded travelers to solve a riddle on pain of death. **Creon**, who was reigning temporarily in Laius's stead, had issued a proclamation which said that he would yield the throne and his sister, Iocasta, to anyone who could solve the riddle and save the city from the sphinx.

Oedipus went to the sphinx and she posed him the riddle: "What creature goes on four legs a dawn, two at midday and three at sunset?" Oedipus answered that it was man, who crawls in his dawn as an infant, walks upright in his midday and hobbles with a stick in his sunset. In her rage at being outwitted, the sphinx hurled herself off the cliff to her death. At this Oedipus went to Thebes, was acclaimed king by the grateful people and married **Iocasta** by whom he had four children: **Eteocles**, **Polynices**, **Antigone** and **Ismene**.

Mysteriously, a plague descended on Thebes and a messenger was sent to consult the Delphic Oracle, returning with the pronouncement that the murderer of Laius had to be expelled. Oedipus ransacked the city to find the culprit but it was only with the reluctant aid of the blind seer **Teiresias**, the most renowned prophet of his time,that the horrible truth dawned on him that he himself was the man he sought.

Iocasta, unable to bear the pain, killed herself and Oedipus, taking the pins from her costume, put out his own eyes.

Blind and driven out from his city he wandered with his daughter Antigone until he reached **Colonus** in Attica where they were afforded protection by its

Top right: Sphynx from a pot, 480 B.C. New York.
Centre: Antigone and the blind Oedipus leaving Thebes. Antoni Stanislaw Brodowski

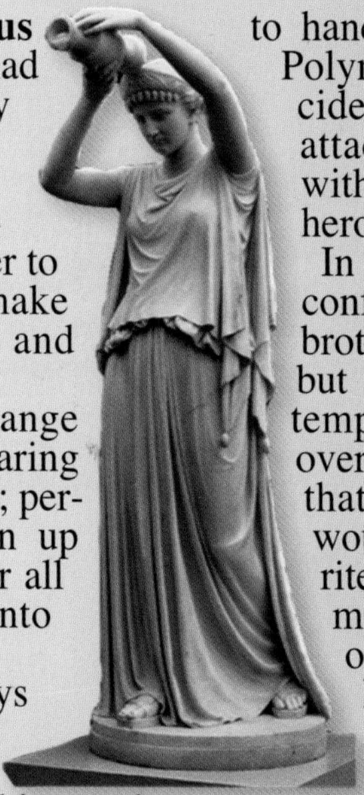

king, **Thesseus** after Oedipus had told him a holy secret which, if it were to be passed down securely from father to son, would make Athens great and strong.

He had a strange ending, disappearing rather than dying; perhaps being taken up by the gods, after all his suffering, into the skies.

Sophocles' plays "**Oedipus Rex**" and "**Oedipus at Colonus**" tell this tragic story which was drawn on as the basis of Freud's theory of the **Oedipus Complex**.

Seven against Thebes

After Oedipus's expulsion and death, the throne of Thebes was taken by his two sons, **Eteocles** and **Polyneices**, who agreed to take it in turn to rule for a year each. First Eteocles reigned while Polyneices was away in Argos at the court of King **Adrastos**. When the year had passed, however, Eteocles refused to hand over power to Polyneices, who decided to launch an attack on Thebes, with the aid of seven heroes.

In the midst of the conflict both of the brothers were killed but Creon, who had temporarily taken over power, declared that only Eteocles would be given the rites of burial, commanding, on pain of death, that Polyneices' body should be left unburied, the prey of wolves and kites, for attacking his homeland.

This story is told in the play "**Seven against Thebes**" by Aeschylus.

Antigone

The tragic story continues with that of **Antigone** who refused to leave the body of her brother, **Polyneices**, unburied, because it was a transgression of unwritten sacred law. So she came into conflict with Creon

Top: Antigone making offerings at the grave of her brother, Polynieces. Rinehart William Henry. Bottom right: The deaths of Eteocles and Polynieces.

Top left: Antigone and Ismene. Emil Teschedorff.
Centre: The torture of Tantalus. Gioacchino Assereto, 1600 – 1649.
Bottom left: Hippodamia offering water to Oinomaios before the expedition with Pelops. Louvre, Paris.

(powerfully portrayed in the Sophoclean' play named after her) and, after she argued her case, buried Polyneices, thereby incurring the death penalty.

Before taking this step, Antigone had asked for help from her sister, **Ismene**, but although she was in agreement with her, the frightened Ismene backed off from lending assistance in the burial of her brother, thus revealing the weakness of her character.

After Antigone died, buried alive in Polyneice's tomb, Creon's son, **Haemon**, who was engaged to her, killed himself

together with his mother. When he learnt what had happened to his son and wife, Creon himself committed suicide Even Ismene, who after these events had become a priestess of Athena, when she was found to have descrated Athina's temple by making love in it with **Polycleimenos**, was killed by the furious goddess. With that death the curse on the **House of Labdacus** finally came to an end.

MYTHS OF THE PELOPONNESE

TANTALUS, PELOPS HOUSE OF ATREUS

A third, but equally rich, cycle of tragic myths are those of the lords of the Peloponnese, on which a host of tragedies were based.

The curse that sets in motion the cycle of myths, begins with **Tantalos**, son of **Zeus** and **Pluto** (Plenty), who was so beloved by the gods that he was allowed to dine with them , but was so insatiable that he stole **Nectar** and **Ambrosia** from the table and secreted them in his palace.

His most frightful act, however, was a kind of macabre test to see whether he could fool the gods. He killed his own son, **Pelona**, ground him up and had him served to the gods who, naturally, weren't so easily fooled. Only Dimitra, pensive and sad for the loss of her daughter, ate one portion. In order to punish Tantalus for this wicked crime Zeus struck him with lightning and banished his soul to the Underworld to be eternally tortured with thirst and hunger, the water in which he stands always falling when he wants to drink and the fruit above his head being whisked away whenever he wants to eat, the so-called "**Torture of Tantallus**".

Centre: The wedding of Hippodamia and Pelops. Mosaic from Olympia. Bottom right: Thyestes takes the infant Aegisthus in his arms.

The gods resurrected **Pelops**, after they had gathered the bits of his body together, and brought him to Ilida in the Peloponnese where he fell deeply in love with **Hippodameia**, daughter of King **Oenomaus**, son of Ares, who, however didn't want her to marry on account of a prophecy that said that his daughter's wedding would bring about his own death. So he challenged each of the suitors to a chariot race, saying that whoever beat him could marry his daughter. But what they didn't know was that the weapons he bore as

well as his two immortal horses had been given him by his father, Ares, and rendered him invincible. So he managed to wipe out all competition.

Pelops colluded with **Myrtilo**, Oenomaus's charioteer, who was also secretly in love with Hippodameia, to remove the lynch-pins from the axles of Oenomaus's chariot so that it overturned, killing him. Before he died, though, he managed to throw a curse on Myrtilo; that he would die at the hands of Pelops, which actually came about when Pelops, catching him in an attempt to ravish Hippodameia, threw him into the sea and drowned him. But in so doing another curse was added to the others, because Myrtilo was the son of **Hermes** who was so outraged at this act that the cursed all of the **House of Pelops** to eternal torment.

Later, after expiating his crime, Pelops became the master of the whole of the Peloponnese, thus giving it its name. He is also considered to be the founder of the Olympic Games.

By Hippodameia he had many children, including **Pittheus**, grandfather of Theseus, **Atreus** and **Thyestes** and an illegitimate son, **Crysippus**, who he doted on, but was killed by his brothers who feared that he would be chosen by their father as his heir.

Pelops, in his pain and fury, added yet another curse to those heaped on his house and started to hunt them down: Atreus and Thyestes took shelter with their sister **Nicippe**, who had married **Sthenelos**, the King of Mycenae. When his son Euristheus (see chapter on Heracles) was killed, the title to the throne passed to the oldest of Pelops's sons, Atreus. However, Thyestes lusted both for his brother's power and for his wife, **Aerope**, and when Atreas got wind of that he devised a most macabre revenge, inviting his brother to a feast at which the roasted flesh of his own children was served (**The Thyestian Banquet**).

By the time that Thyestes realized the horror of what had been done it was too late; he had eaten his children. The only refuge he had was to consult the Delphic Oracle which delivered him another puzzling prediction: that he would have a son by his own daughter who would bring the House of Atreus to an end.

In fact that was just what happened; from Atreus's incestuous relationship with his daughter, **Pelopia**, was born **Aegisthus** who his ashamed mother abandoned in the Arcadian mountains and who was at first looked after by the shepherds who chanced upon him, then reclaimed by his father who had somehow learned of his whereabouts, and reared as his heir.

Further on we will learn of the role that Aegisthus played in the House of Atreus after he had murdered Atreus and installed Thyestes on the throne.

But before Menelaus took Helen to be his bride, the greatest princes of the time had competed for her heart, swearing an oath that whoever prevailed would always guard the marriage. When Menelaus emerged as victor they were already bound by an oath that would lead to the greatest of all ancient military expeditions.

The House of the Atreids

Atreus and Merope had two sons, **Agamemnon** and **Menelaos**, who, for fear of Thyestes, took shelter with **Tyndareus**, the King of Sparta, who helped Agamemnon regain the throne of **Mycenae**. Agamemnon made Mycenae one of the richest and strongest cities of that time (about 1300-1200 B.C.).an important source of which was the help he had given the Egyptians in resisting the raids of the Hyksos, which was so richly rewarded that Mycenae received the epithet "**Golden**".

Tyndareus gave his daughter **Clytemnestra** to Agamnenon as his wife, while to Tyndareus he gave another daughter, the beautiful Helen who, since her brothers the Dioscuroi were dead, had as her dowry the Kingdom of **Sparta**.

Agamemnon and Clytemnestra had three children: **Iphigenia**, **Electra** and **Orestes** on whom the fate of their House so heavily weighed that they were subsequently made the subjects of some of the greatest Greek tragedies.

THE TROJAN WAR

THE ABDUCTION OF HELEN

THE SACRIFICE OF IPHIGENIA

THE WAR

THE DEATH OF ACHILLES

THE WOODEN HORSE

THE FALL OF TROY

THE TROJAN WAR

The Trojan War was the greatest clash between the **Achaians**; those who lived in Greece, and the **Trojans** of Asia Minor, who shared a common language, religion and customs and so must be considered Greeks. In essence it was a ten-year civil war which passed into the Greek collective consciousness through the **Homeric Epics**.

The historicality of what Homer described was proved by **Heinrich Schliemann** who, following exactly Homer's descriptions, found the site of Troy and unearthed the ninth layer, destroyed by fire in about 1200 B.C, as well as many other Mycenaen remains.

The underlying cause of the war was the desire of the Achaians to dominate the fertile area of Troy, mainland Greece being mountainous with few plains.

The Judgment of Paris

Nearly all the gods had been invited to the wedding of **Peleus**, King of Phthias in Thessaly, with the Nereid **Thetis**, the exception being **Eris**, the goddess of discord. In reprisal Eris found a way to create mischief leading to great ruin.

When the wedding feast was underway she cast down a golden apple on which was written "**For the most beautiful.**" Three beautiful goddesses contended for this title. Zeus, being unable to set-

Top: Some of the protagonists in the Trojan War. From the left: Menelaus, Paris, Diomedes, Nestor, Agamemnon, Achilles and Odysseus.

tle the issue, sent the three, together with Hermes, to Mount Ida, near Troy, where **Paris** was called upon to give judgment.

Each of them: **Hera**, **Athena** and **Aphrodite**, spoke to Paris in turn, offering him inducements to choose them. Athena offered wisdom and courage in war, Hera strength and power over all of Asia and Aphrodite the beautiful **Helen** to be his wife. Naturally the young man chose the beautiful woman and gave the apple to Aphrodite and it was this that set off a chain of events that was to lead to the greatest war in Greek mythology.

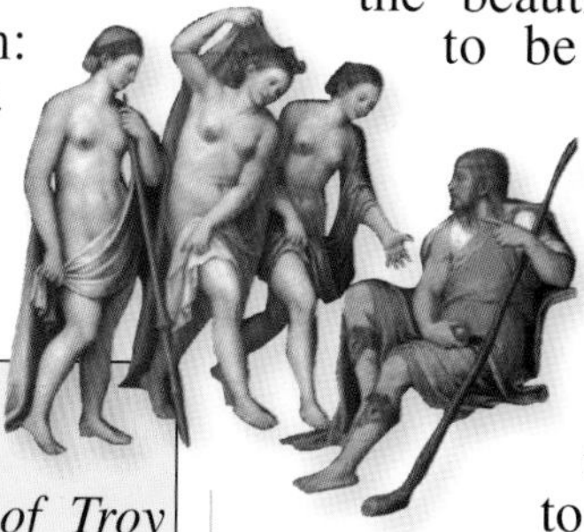

__Paris__ was one of the fifty sons of __Priam__, King of Troy and __Hecuba__ who, in childbirth, saw in a vision that she was giving birth to a flaming torch that would set fire to Troy. The alarmed parents ordered the infant to be taken to Mount Ida and exposed there for the wild animals to tear apart. But a shepherd, coming across the child, took pity on it and reared it to be a shepherd. But Fate had decided otherwise.

Centre: The judgment of Paris. Juan de Juanes, 1523 – 1579. Bottom right: The same subject, this time by Giordano Luca, 1632 – 1705.

The Abduction of Helen

Helen lived and ruled with **Menelaus** in Sparta and they had a daughter, **Hermione**. When the time for fulfilling her promise had come, Aphrodite led **Paris** to Sparta where he was received and hosted by Menelaus in a way befitting a prince.

After a few days, however, he was obliged to leave for Crete, to attend the funeral of his grandfather, Catreus, and Helen, smitten with love for Paris, seizing the opportunity, left with him for Troy, abandoning her daughter and taking with her all her riches.

Returning from Crete and finding that he had been betrayed, Menelaus sent messengers to the princes and kings of Greece, calling on them to fulfill the oaths they had sworn to protect his marriage. So was preparation for the **Trojan Campaign** started on the pretext of defending Menelaus's honour.

The Gathering at Aulis

Soon they started to organize an army and to build ships, the preparations centering on **Aulis** in Boiotia. This grew to an enormous military strength, with numerous ships and men drawn from nearly every part of Greece,

Top: Helen of Troy. Evelyn De Morgan, 1898. Bottom: the abduction of Helen. Giordano Luca, 1634 – 1705.

Top: Hector, Paris and Helen. Pierre Claud Francoise Delrome, 1783 – 1859. Below: Achilles, dressed as a woman,betrays his true nature by chosing a spear from among Odysseus's gifts. Painting by Pompeo Batoni (1745).

Other related myths should be mentioned here:

The prophet **Chalcus**, the official seer of the expedition, had predicted that in order to win the war they would have to take the young **Achilles**, son of Peleus, with them. Thetis, his mother, had tried to make him immortal by plunging the child into the sacred **waters of Styx**, keeping hold of him by the ankle. So was it that Achilles's body was invulnerable except at that point (**Achiles's heel**).

Afterwards he was sent to be reared by **Cheiron** the **Centaur** on Mount Pelion who taught him, apart from other things, the martial arts for which he would be famed.

But Thetis, in order to prevent him from taking part in the war, concealed him in the court of King **Lycomedes** on Skyros where he was dressed in women's clothing and played with the king's daughters.

But **Odysseus**, the King of Ithaca, getting wind of this subterfuge, and, dressed as a trader, approached the children, having put among his goods a wooden sword and shield which, of course, Achilles grabbed, revealing his identity and accepting to take part in the war, together with King Phthia's warriors, the famed **Myrmidons**.

*But **Odysseus** himself had already thought of escaping the war by playing the madman. So when the representatives called to invite his participation, they found that he had yoked an ox to a horse and, dressed in a funny hat, was sowing salt instead of seed. Then **Palamides**, son of Navplion, threw Odysseus's new-born son, **Telemacus**, in front of the plough, naturally enough obliging the hero to stop, thus betraying the fact that he was not mad and obliging him to promise to take part.*

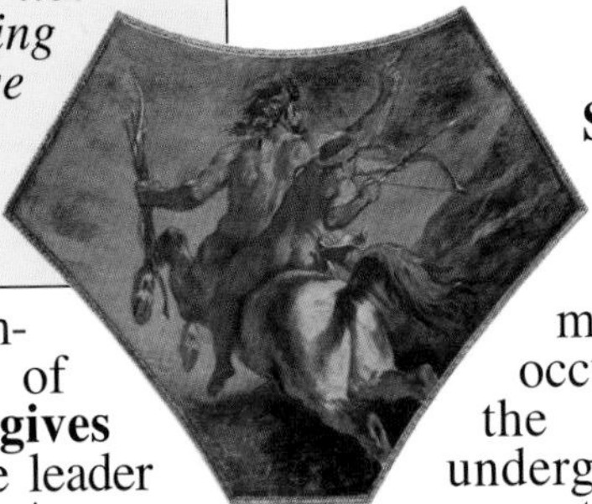

under the common names of **Achaians**, **Argives** or **Danaoi**. The leader they chose was **Agamemnon**, king of the strongest state at that time, **Mycenae**, which also had the largest army. But the bravest and most skilled in martial arts was **Achilles** and the most inventive and intelligent, **Odysseus**.

So numerous are the names of those who took part in the expedition that it would be tedious to list them, but whichever of

them were involved in different episodes will be referred to as the story unfolds.

The Sacrifice of Iphigenia

The first misfortune occurred while the fleet was undergoing final preparations at Aulis. On a hunt, Agamemnon entered a forest sacred to **Artemis** and killed one of the **sacred deer**. The angry goddess thus prevented the favourable winds the fleet needed from blowing.

The seer **Chalcas**, who was part of the force, pronounced that Artemis would never be appeased unless the first born daughter of Agamemnon, **Iphige-**

***Top left**: Iphigenia, by Anselm Feuerbach, 1862*
***Centre left**: Chairon. Eugene Delacroix, 1798 – 1863.*
***Bottom left**: Chalkas the seer.*
***Right**: The sacrifice of Iphigenia. Wall painting from Pompeii, 4th C. B.C. Naples.*
***Bottom**: Achilles and Ajax playing dice. Hydria, 490 B.C.*

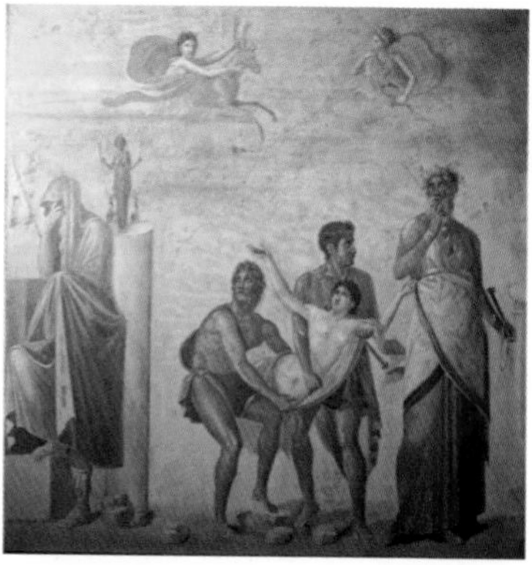

nia, were sacrificed.

Though at first Agamemnon refused to listen to this advice, in the end he was forced to take it because of the restiveness of those waiting to set out. Following Odysseus's advice he sent a message to his wife, **Clytemenestra**, asking her to send Iphigenia to Aulis to be married to Achileas.

When the two happy women arrived at Aulis the sacrifice had already been prepared and they soon learnt the truth. Clytemnestra's smiles turned to furious curses but Iphigenia, seeing that it was for the common good, showing great nobility of spirit, offered herself voluntarily up for sacrifice.

But at the very moment that Chalcas raised the sacrificial knife, **Artemis**, taking pity on the innocent child, wrapped the altar in a cloud and bore her away to Taurid to serve as her priestess, leaving a deer in her place. Once the sacrifice had taken place the winds began to blow to carry the ships to Troy.

This story is told in Euripides' moving play "Iphigenia"

The Trojan War

Homer's **Iliad**, called after the alternative name for Troy, Illium, starts in the tenth year of the war, after a long drawn-out series of bloody skirmishes and battles had reached stalemate and the siege of Troy dragged on.

Top right: Agamemnon's representatives visit Achilles's tent to ask for Chrysida. Jean Auguste Dominique Ingres. 1801.

The Olympian gods took part in this struggle on both sides, helping their favoured ones. Those particularly distinguished in battle were, on the Achaian side, **Achilles**, **Ajax**, son of **Telemon**, **Ajax** the

Locrian, Achille's close friend **Patroclus**, **Idomeneus** King of Crete, the crafty and ingenious **Odysseus** and **Diomedes**. While prominent among the Trojans were **Hector**, the eldest son of **Priam**, **Antenor** and **Aeneas**, son of Aphrodite and, later, founder of Rome.

In the tenth year of the war, then, an incident occurred that signified the beginning of the end.

The Greek army had been struck by a sickness sent by Apollo after one of his priests, **Chryses** appealed to him to help him get his daughter, **Chryseis**, back from the Achaens, who had abducted her. Chalcas the seer prophesied that only if the girl was returned would the sickness cease.

Chryseis, however, had become **Agamemnon's** concubine and although he reluctantly agreed to send her back he resolved to cut his losses by exploiting his position and taking Achille's concubine, **Briseis**, instead.

The two men fell out so

Centre: Achilles and Agamemnon ready to fight over Brysida.. Bottom right: Brysida being conveyed to Agamemnon's tent. Tiepolo.

badly that Achilles, seeing there was no way he could get Briseis back, decided that after such an insult there was no way that he and his myrmidons could continue to take part in the fighting. This is the famous "**Wrath of Achilles**" mentioned in the first rhapsody of the Iliad.

Without Achilles, the Achaens were extremely vulnerable, repeatedly losing battles. The Trojans, under the brave leadership of their chief, Hector, breaking out of Troy decimated them, even reaching the Greek fleet, which they nearly managed to burn. In vain they tried to persuade Achilles to help them, because they were at risk of losing everything. Achilles's mother, **Thetis**, had even persuaded the gods to turn a deaf ear to the Achaeans' pleas, until they showed their esteem for her son.

At this point of deadlock, Achille's bosom friend, **Patroclus**, enters the tale, persuading him to lend him the famous armour wrought by Hephaestus so that the Trojans would be fooled into thinking that Achilles had returned to battle. So the hero, after receiving satisfaction from Agamemnon who apologized and returned Briseis to him, handed over his army to Patroclus who went out and fought in his stead.

When the Trojans beheld what they thought to be Achilles fighting with great valour, they fled, with great loss, back to the walls of Troy. Patroclus, in the heat of his anger reached right to

Top: Achilles takes care of the wounded Patroclus. Kylix,work of Sosias, 5th C. B.C. Centre: Either Menalaos or Ajax, son of Telemon, supporting the body of Patroclus. Bottom, right: Achilles in single combat with Penthesilea, Queen of the Amazons.

the city gates where, however, **Hector**, who had been informed by Apollo of the warrior's true identity, confronted and killed him.

A **Homeric battle** – as it is still called – was fought over Patroclus's body, during which Hector managed to get possession of Achilles's armour, both **Ajax Telamon** and **Antilochos** also fighting bravely. It was Antilochos, though, who had to take the tragic news back to Achilles.

Achilles, demented by grief, after he had overseen the burning of his young friend's body according to custom and with every honour, organized games in his memory; the "**Patrocleia**".

Claiming vengeance he decided to enter the war and to kill Hector, scorning the oracle that said that his own death would follow hard on that of Hector. He asked for a new suit of armour from his mother, forged and crafted by **Hephaestus**.

Centre: Hector bids farewell to Andromache and his son, Astynax. Krater, 370 B.C.
Bottom: Thetis brings new weapons to the grieving Achilles. Benjamin West, 1806.

The description of his shield in the "Patrocleia" rhapsody is one of the most famous passages in world literature.

Achilles entered the battle, scattering death among thousands of Trojans, always on the watch for Hector. The scene between Hector and **Andromache**, his wife in which, with their child in her arms she tries to persuade him not to go out to fight in single combat with Achilles is one of the most moving in the poem.

But, in the end, Hector went out and met his foe at the **Scayan Gates**. The account of their combat is unforgettable and ends with the death of Hector, whose body Achilles, in unappeasable rage, ties to his chariot and desecrates it by dragging it around the walls before leaving it to

lie unburied.

There follows another extremely moving episode as **Prium**, the aged King of Troy, dressed simply, manages to get to Achilles's tent and with tears in his eyes kisses the hands of the man who killed his son and pleads him to give up the body for burial. Recognizing Priam's magnanimity and nobility of character, Achilles treats him with respect, yields him the

Top right: Priam begs Achilles to give him the body of his son, Hector.
Centre: The same scene interpreted by Alexander Ivanov, 1806 – 1858.
Bottom: Achilles's triumph. Franz von Maz. Achileos, Corfu.

body and declares an armistice so that the body can be buried with the honour befitting such a valiant warrior.

The Death of Achilles

The war continued, Achilles scattering death among the Trojans and accomplishing such unparalleled feats that they were obliged to man the walls continually. But his fate was prescribed. Apollo advised **Paris** to join the battle and, when he got close to Achilles, to fire a poisoned arrow at the only vulnerable part of his body, his heel. And so the greatest hero of the war died. His body, over which a battle raged, was finally recovered by **Odysseus**, with the aid of **Ajax**, and carried to the Greek camp. Mourning and tributes to him lasted seventeen days, his body kept from corruption by the preservative oils by his mother and sisters, the **Nereids**. After the body was burnt on a pyre, the ashes were put, together with those of Patroclus, in an amphora which was buried in a great funeral mound.

Achilles had had a son in Skyros, when he was very young: ***Neoptolemus****, who, when he had grown up also played an important part in the Trojan expedition, since it had been prophesied that his presence was necessary for Troy to be occupied.*

After rival claims among the rescuers of Achilles's body, Ajax and Odysseus, his armour was awarded to Odysseus. Paris, who Homer showed little respect for as being lacking in manly courage, soon met his death at the hands of **Philoctetes**.

Philoctetus was armed with the weapons of Hercules which he had given him shortly before he died (see chapter on Heracles's downfall). After he had set out on the Trojan expedition, at one of the stops, on Lemnos, he was bitten by a snake, a

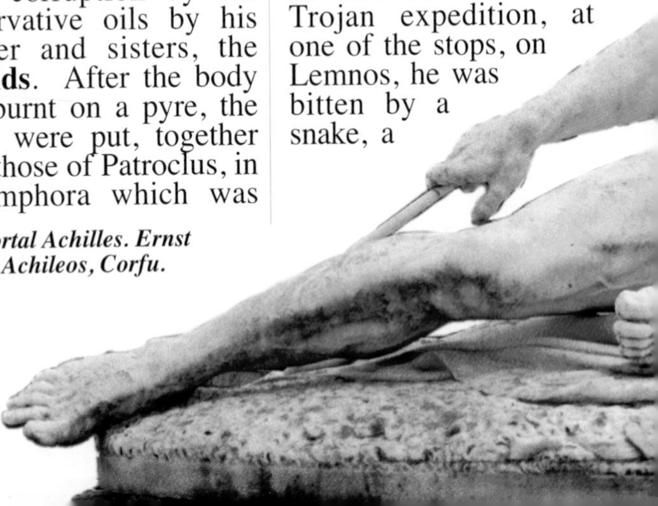

The mortal Achilles. Ernst Herter. Achileos, Corfu.

Alexander the Great at the tomb of Achilles, before his expedition into Asia.
.. "If only I had the luck, son of Thetida, to be hymned, as you were, by Homer" he wished.

wound that festered. His companions, unable to bear his cries and the stink, abandoned him on the island, where he stayed for nine years – until Odysseus learnt from the seer **Elenos**, son of Priam, that Troy would fall only if the Achaians possessed Heracles's bow and arrows.

Odysseus went to Limnos and, by some subterfuge, stole the weapons from Philoctetus who, rather than stay on the island without any means to hunt, followed him to Troy where, after being treated by **Machaonas**, son of Asclepius, he re entered the fray, achieving much.

But since this war promised to be interminable, Odysseus, with the collaboration of his guardian goddess Athina, conceived a trick to finally defeat the city.

Top right: Casssandra. Max Klinger, 1857 – 1920. Bottom: Lacoon and his two sons in the coils of a sea-serpent. Roman copy of the 1st C. A.D. of an original by the Rhodian sculptor, Agisandros. Vatican Museum.

The Wooden Horse

They constructed a **wooden horse** big enough to contain hundred of men in its hollow insides and in-scribed on it that it was dedicated to Athena and the Danaens. After the best fighters had hidden themselves inside it they left it

in a prominent position, burnt their encampment, put out to sea in their ships and anchored behind the nearby island of **Tenedos**.

When the Trojans saw the Danaens withdrawing they couldn't believe their eyes and cautiously approached the wooden horse. They then decided to take it into the town in thanksgiving to the goddess who had delivered them from war.

In vain the seer **Cassandra**, Priam's daughter, warned that the horse contained great danger. No one believed her. (see chapter on Oracles) And when **Lacoon**, priest of Apollo, hurled his spear at the horse and from the noise it made when it struck understood that it was hollow, warned them to **beware of the**

Top right: Neoptolemos kills Priam in front of the statue of Zeus. French. 17th C.
Centre: Ajax carries off Cassandra. Solomon Joseph Solomon, 1860 – 1927.
Bottom left: Troy burning. Pieter Schoubroeck, 1570 – 1607.
Bottom right: The wooden horse of Troy.

Danaens, even when bearing gifts.

At this Athena sent from the sea two huge snakes that crushed Lacoon and his sons to death.

When they had dragged the huge offering into the city they launched a great celebration in sheer relief at the end of this terrible war. When all had at last fallen silent, the Achaian warriors stole out of the horse and opened the gates to let in the rest who had returned in their ships undetected, under cover of night. Then the slaughter of the unprepared population began. **Neoptolemus** slaughtered **Priam** on the altar of Zeus and hurled his son **Astynax** from the battlements. The Achaens raged unchecked, raping, pillaging, destroying and after taking the most beautiful and prominent women into slavery, they burnt the once shining city.

One myth says that when Menelaos found Helen, he

Ajax's suicide.
Kalyx, 4th C. B.C.

took out his sword to kill her but she, quite unafraid, bared her breasts and her betrayed husband, unable to resist her beauty, was reconciled to her, took her on board his ship and, after many adventures, returned with her to Sparta.

Euripedes's play "The Trojans" tells of the fate of the enslaved Trojan women, after the fall of Troy.

So ended a war that shook the ancient Greek world and had repercussions down the centuries, especially through its portrayal in literature and art.

But because many outrages had been committed by the Achaens during the sack of Troy, most of them came to a bad end, many ships being lost on the return voyage, disaster overtaking them.

But the worst-fated of all were Agamemnon and Odysseus, the first to be murdered by his wife, and the second to wander over the seas for ten years, blown this way and that, before finally reaching home.

***Ajax**, son of **Telamon** the King of Salamina was one of the most important figures in the Trojan expedition. Homer relates how, when he was born, Heracles wrapped him in his lion-skin, thus rendering his whole body invincible, except for his armpits.*

His courage in Homeric battles was legendary. When he fought man-to-man with Hector and they reached stalemate, the two combatants exchanged gifts in recognition of the other's worthiness and courage. In the wild battle that raged over Patroclus's body he came out on top and managed to seize the body and carry it back to the Greek camp.

After Achilles's death, during the commemorative games, it was decided to award his weapons to the bravest Greek. And when Odysseus was given unjust preferment, Ajax, driven mad with rage, grabbed a sword and stabbed himself to death.

Agamemnon's Return The End of the House of Atreus

With the return of Agamemnon to **Mycenae** the curse on the house of Atreus continues to unfold. **Clytemnestra**, his wife, had been nursing her hatred of him ever since he ordered the sacrifice of their daughter Iphigenia at Aulis, and thirsted for revenge. At the same time she was having an affair with his cousin, **Aegisthus** (see chapter on the House of Atreus), the two of them sharing power. She had taken the precaution of sending her son **Orestes** to the court of the King of Phocida, so as not to be a witness to her adultery, while treating her daughter **Electra** (under pressure from Aegisthus) as a slave.

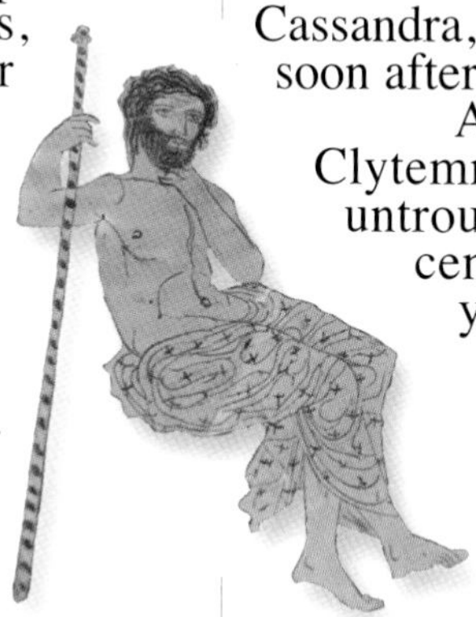

Clytemenestra feigned joy at Agamemnon's return, even though he brought **Cassandra** with him as his lover, and prepared a luxurious bath for him and it was there that she and Aegisthus cast a net over him and slaughtered him. Then they turned their attention to Cassandra, murdering her soon after.

Aegisthus and Clytemnestra ruled untroubled at Mycenae for eight years until Orestes, now a grown man, having learnt what had happened to his father, set out with his bosom friend **Pylades**, son of the King of Phocida, with the aim of taking revenge.

When he reached **Argos** he chanced to come across his sister Electra

Centre: Agamemnon. Attic lekani, 4th C. B.C. Bottom: Clytemnestra hesitating to kill her husband. Pierre Narcisse Guerin. 1774 – 1833.

Top right: The golden "mask of Agamemnon" discovered at Mycenae by Heinrich Schliemann. National Museum, Athens. In fact the mask is much older dating from the 12th C. B.C.

lamenting the death of her father, the loss of her brother and her own hard fate. Naturally enough she, at first, did not recognize him, but when she did her joy knew no bounds. Together now they plotted their revenge. Orestes was at first daunted at the enormity of the task ahead but, urged on by Electra, managed to kill Aegisthus. But fate had more in store.

Clytemnestra, in her attempt to defend her lover from her son, ran at him with an axe and he, while attempting to defend himself, unintentionally killed her. Even though right was on his side, Orestes had committed the great sin of matricide and so, from the moment of his mother's death, he started to be pursued by the **Erinies** (deities of guilt), driving him to the edge of madness. Seeking shelter at the Delphic Oracle he was told to go to Athens to be tried by the **Areopagus** (High Court) where his plea of innocence was accepted, with Athina's decisive vote. Returning to Mycenae he resumed the throne, while his friend Pylades married his sister, Electra.

There is, however, another interesting ver-

Middle: Clytemenestra holding a sword. Painiting by John Colier.
Bottom left: Orestes kills Aegisthus and Clytemnestra. Bernardino Mei, 1654.

sion of this myth which says that when Orestes consulted the Oracle at Delphi for advice he was told that in order to purify himself from the miasma of matricide he would have to bring back to Greece the xoana (wooden effigy) of **Artemis** from **Tauris** on the Black Sea. Unknown to him, however, the high priestess of that temple was **Iphigenia**, who had been saved, at the last minute, from sacrifice by the goddess (see chapter: The Gathering at Aulis).

In Tauris, a barbaric country, they honoured the goddess by sacrificing whatever foreigner came their way on her altar. When Orestes and Pylades reached there it was Iphigenia's task to purify them in preparation for their sacrifice. Learning where they had come from she asked them about the fate of her family. There followed a most moving recognition. Iphigenia decided to help Orestes deceive the King of Tauris.

So the miasma and **curse** of the House of Atreus, torn apart by domestic crime and violence, was finally purged.

Apart from the Greek tragic poets who wrote many plays on this theme, it inspired many European artists and writers, including Racine and Goethe, who wrote his own "Iphigenia auf Tauris", and musicians such as **Gluck** who wrote many operas based on Greek myths.

Top right: Orestes and Pylades. Francois Bouchot, 1800 – 1842.
Centre: Electra at the tomb of Agamemnon. William Blake Richmond, 1874.
Bottom: Orestes and the Erynies. Adolph William Bouguereau.

THE ODYSSEY

ODYSSEUS

The second of Homer's great epics, which refers to Odysseus's adventures after the end of the Trojan War, is the Odyssey, a work which, according to the experts, is much more mature, both as a narrative and in relation to its content, which is not just much closer to the nature of Greeks but, in general, to human nature.

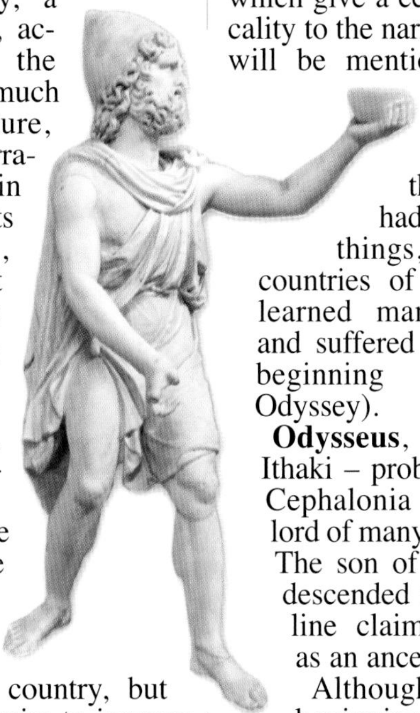

It is the story of the fervent desire of a man to return to his country, but also of his desire to journey and discover new places.

Odysseus is an epitome of the Greek character: curious, exploratory, crafty, inventive, persistent and brave and (as Homer calls him) resourceful. Yet he always has his aim in sight: to return to his homeland, his family and his wife, Penelope, that symbol of faithfulness.

On his ten year-journey Odysseus passed through many different regions which give a certain historicality to the narration. These will be mentioned as we come to them in this tale of the "man who had done many things, seen the countries of many men, learned many opinions and suffered much." (the beginning of the Odyssey).

Odysseus, King of Ithaki – probably today's Cephalonia – was the lord of many Ionian isles. The son of **Laertes**, he descended from a great line claiming Hermes as an ancestor.

Although at the beginning he didn't want to take part in the Trojan Expedition, in the event his intelligence,

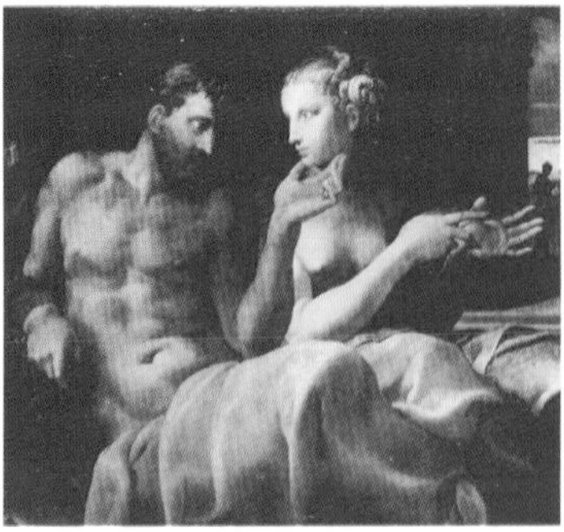

Centre: Odysseus as a beggar. Ciaramonti Museum. Bottom right: Odysseus and Penelope. Francesco Primaticcio, 1563.

resourcefulness and inventiveness proved to be especially valuable. He it was who found answers to the knottiest problems, the inventor of the wooden horse by means of which the Danaens overthrew Troy. It was he, too, who undertook the most delicate diplomatic missions.

Though the Odyssey does contain historic elements that have been subsequently confirmed, it is chiefly a work of poetic imagination which has stayed in people's memories as the narration of the greatest adventure undertaken in antiquity.

The Land of the Cyconians

After the destruction of Troy the returning Achaian fleet was scattered by a great storm and those of Odysseus, separated from the rest, arrived at the land of the **Cyconians** on the coast of Thrace.

There they joined battle with the natives, from which they emerged victorious and sacked and pillaged the town, including the Temple of Apollo, for which they were punished by the god with the loss of nine men from every boat. The only respect they showed was to Apollo's priest, **Maro**, who presented them with twelve jars of holy wine.

The Lotus-eaters

Setting sail again and heading towards Cytherea they were blown completely off-course again for nine days, until they reached the coast of North Africa, perhaps at an island called Djerba, in Tunisia where they were well-received by the local people who offered them a wonderful fruit, the **lotus**. The moment they had eaten it, however, all desire to return to their homeland was wiped out. Only by force did Odysseus manage to tear his companions away from the land of the Lotus-eaters to

Centre: Penelope with Odysseus's bow. R.S. Wyatt, 1795 – 1850.
Bottom left: Maronas offers Odysseus a wine-sack.

continue their journey back north, towards Sicily, where they came across the Isle of the Cyclops.

The Cyclops

The Cyclops were monstrous beings with just one eye in the middle of their foreheads and were mainly occupied in herding. They were, according to the myth, sons of the god **Poseidon** and were uninhibitedly wild in their behaviour. Unwittingly, Odysseus landed on the island to replenish his stocks. It was while he and his men were feasting in a cave that the man-eating **Polyphemus** waylaid them, blocking the entrance and drawing on them as a food-supply, eating one a day and closing the entrance with a huge stone each night.

It was then that Odysseus hit on a plan of escape, making use of the fact that every evening Polyphemus shut his sheep up in the cave with them and let them free in the morning.

One evening Odysseus offered Polyphemus one of the jars of holy wine he had been given by Maro, in reward, as he said, for the hospitality shown to them. Accepting the gift, the giant asked the name of his guest and Odysseus answered that he was called Oudeis "**nobody**". Polyphemus enjoyed the wine and, naturally, asked for more, which he was given in great quantity.

When the drunken monster had fallen into a stupor Odysseus's companions fetched the huge pointed wooden stake they had kept flaming on the fire and thrust it into Polyphemus's only eye. Polyphemus's terrible cries roused the other Cyclops who, when they asked him what had happened, were told that he had been blinded by "nobody". Seeing this as some huge joke they left him howling and furious.

Centre: Odysseus offers the Cyclops Marona's wine.

When he rolled back the stone to let his sheep out next morning, he groped around to find his attackers. But Odysseus had tied his men to the bellies of the rams, the middle one of three, and thus all escaped, himself last of all, hanging onto the fleece under the largest ram.

Immediately they reached

the ships they were taken on board by their comrades and set off with the greatest speed they could muster. But Odysseus couldn't resist shouting to Polyphemus that "no one" was Odysseus, King of Ithaca, in reply to which the monster hurled a huge stone which smashed into the sea close to the ship and cursed Odysseus, in the name of his father, Poseidon, to

be a wanderer over the sea, reaching his homeland late and alone. And this was Odysseus's fate for the next ten years.

Aeolus

Odysseus's next stop was in **Aeolia**, an iron-walled island belonging to the god of the winds, **Aeolus**, who hosted them hospitably for a month, shutting up all the winds in his sack (Aeolus's sack) apart from Zephyrus, the west wind, that they would need for their journey. Giving him the sack, the god told Odysseus not to open it on any account.

For nine days they were blown by this favouring wind until they nearly reached Ithaca, their homeland. But, suspecting that there was some sort of treasure in the bag, Odysseus's companions took and opened it while he was sleeping and out flew all the winds with great turbulence, blowing the ship back to Aeolia. Odysseus pleaded with Aeolus to calm the storm and send a favourable wind again, but, seeing that by so doing he would be going against the will of the gods, he refused and abandoned the hero to his fate.

The Laestrygones

Continuing the journey they reached the land of the **Laestrygones**, inhabited by wild, cannibalistic giants who, as soon as they saw the companions, rushed at them and started to eat them. Terrified, the men ran for their ships and tried to turn them out to sea, but the

Above: Odysseus and his companions prepare to conceal themselves beneath Polyphemus's sheep. Jacob Jordaens, 1650. Bottom right: The blinding of the Cyclops. Amphora, 650 B.C.

Top right: Polyphemus hurls a rock at Odysseus's ship. John Flaxman, 1810. National Gallery, Washington.
Bottom: Circe toasts Odysseus. John William Waterhouse.

Laestrygones hurled enormous boulders at them and sunk them. In the end only Odysseus's ship escaped which, after many tempests and adventures, arrived at Aeaea, the Island of the **Dawn,** possibly Monte Circeo in Italy.

Circe

Circe, the daughter of **Helius** and **Perse**, was a sorceress. When a detachment of Odysseus's men, led by **Eurylochus**, went to meet her she at first treated them with hospitality, but, having lulled them into a false sense of security, raised her wand and changed them into pigs. Eurylochus managed to escape and bring the news to his chief who decided to go and visit her alone, having first taken a potion given to him by

Hermes that would render him invulnerable to her magic. When Circe attempted to cast her spell on him and saw that not only did it not work but that he was threatening her with his sword, she swore that she would do no more harm and, undoing the damage she had done, change his companions back into men.

Odysseus became Circe's lover and stayed with her for a year, having a son by her, **Telegonus**, without, however, forgetting his final goal.

Odysseus in Hades

Respecting his wish to return to his homeland, Circe advised Odysseus to descend into Hades to question the spirit of the seer, **Tiresias**, about his best course of action. Odysseus came to the river Acheron, the entrance to the Underworld and, after digging a trench, sacrificed a

Another piece of advice that Tiresias gave to Odysseus was that he should appease Poseidon in the following strange way: to put an oar on his shoulder and set out to find a place where the inhabitant had no idea what it was. And there he should slaughter a ram, a boar and a bull. Finally, he prophesied that death would come to him from the sea.

Odysseus listens to the advice of Tiriseas, whose headless body can be seen at his feet. Krater, work of Dolona, 4th C. B.C.

black sheep to Pluto and Proserpina. After the spirit of Tiresias had approached and quenched its thirst on the blood, it gave Odysseus a lot of advice, and prophesies such as that he would finally reach home, but in a strange ship, and that other catstrophes would be awaiting him there. Also, that he should care not to bother the oxen of the sun god, Helios, in any way, under any circumstances.

While he was in Hades, Odysseus met with many of the spirits of those that were lost in Troy, one of which was that of **Achilles** who told him that he would prefer to be the most humble of living men rather than to be famous and consigned to Hades. Others he met included Patroclus, Minos, Theseus, Rhadamanthus and Agamemnon, who told him of his tragic fate. But the most moving of his meetings was with his mother, Anticlea, who he didn't know was dead.

The Sirens

After he had returned from Hades, Odysseus began to plan his departure. Circe warned him that he would have to pass by the **Sirens**, creatures with women's heads and birds' bodies who sang so beautifully that whoever heard them was unable

Left: Odysseus and the Sirens. Herbert James Draper, 1909

to resist and, forgetting everything, stayed with them on their island, **Anemoessa** which, however, was so parched and infertile that those bewitched perished slowly from hunger and thirst.

So forewarned, Odysseus ordered his companions to tie him to the mast and plug their ears with wax as soon as the island was sighted, so being able to hear the bewitching song of the sirens without danger of loosing his bonds.

Scylla and Charybdis

Their way now led them through some straits between two precipitous cliffs on which dwelt, on one side **Scylla**, a six-headed monster who tore all within reach to pieces, and, on the other, **Charybdis**, a voracious monster who sucked in huge quantities of seawater three times a day and then spewed it out again.

Following Circe's advice, they steered their ship close to Scylla's side and, rowing for all they were worth, managed to get through with the loss of only six men, one for each head of the monster.

The Cattle of the Sun

Finally they reached **Thrynacius**, an island, dedicated to the sun-god **Helios**, which may have been Sicily. Remembering the advice given him by Tiresias in Hades, not to trouble the god's cattle in any way, Odysseus wanted to leave immediately, but his companions had need of rest. So they came to the agreement that they could go ashore on the understanding that none of them were to bother the cattle.

But the next day a tempest

Top left: Attic stamnos, 480 B.C. British Museum, London.
Bottom: Odysseus and the Sirens. John William Waterhouse, 1861.

arose that was to rage for a month. For as long as the food that Circe had given them lasted they kept their oath. But one day, while Odysseus was away, pleading for the aid of the gods, they took advantage of his absence and slaughtered the finest of the sacred cattle to appease their gnawing hunger. Only Odysseus, on his return, refused to partake in the feast. Thus it was, when the storm fell and they had set out again, that Zeus, to appease the angry sun god, struck the ship with lightning, splitting it in two, only Odysseus, out of all that host, being saved.

Calypso

Tossed about by the waves of the angry sea for nine days Odysseus managed to reach **Ogygia**, the island of **Calypso**, a beautiful nymph, daughter of Atlanta, who looked after him, fell in love with him and became his lover.

For a long time – some say five, others seven years – Odysseus lived under the charm of Calypso who tried to make him forget Ithaca, but the yearning to reach his homeland grew with the passage of time until, one day **Athina**, seeing how depressed he was and sympathizing with him, asked for the assistance of **Zeus** who, taking advantage of **Poseidon's** absence in Ethiopia, sent Hermes to Calypso to announce to her the gods' decision to set the hero free.

With a heavy heart Calypso was obliged to part with her love, after helping him to build a stout raft and equip it with everything necessary for the journey back to his country.

But Odysseus's torments were not to be brought so quickly to an end; when Poseidon, on his journey back, saw him in his raft he raised a huge wave that swept him overboard and shattered the vessel.

Odysseus and Nausicaa

Odysseus was carried by the waves for two days before being swept ashore, half-dead on the island of the Phaeacians – today's Corfu- called **Scheria** by

Centre. Sirens. John William Waterhouse, 1900.

Homer, a vibrant culture in its acme ruled over by Alcinous and Arete who had a daughter, **Nausicaa**,

When Odysseus was thrown up almost lifeless onto the shore he fell into a state of deep unconsciousness from which he was awakened by the sound of girlish laughter, Nausicaa, who had come to wash her linen in the stream, playing ball and her handmaidens. When Odysseus appeared in front of them, enfeebled, trying to hide his nakedness, she pitied him so much she offered him clean clothes and led him to her father's palace.

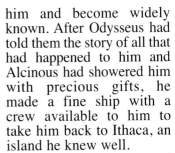

Alcinous welcomed Odysseus to his noble palace and, when he had learned who he was – which is where the "Odyssey" begins – organized celebrations in his honour, his achievements and his fame having preceded him and become widely known. After Odysseus had told them the story of all that had happened to him and Alcinous had showered him with precious gifts, he made a fine ship with a crew available to him to take him back to Ithaca, an island he knew well.

Towards the end of the journey Odysseus fell into a deep sleep from which there was no waking him, so they carried him ashore, leaving him with Alcinous's gifts around him.

Ithaca

After twenty years, at last Odyssseus lay on his native earth. When he awoke he found a shepherd boy in front of him who told him that if he wanted to learn how things were on the island he should visit the shepherd **Eumaios**. The boy then threw off his disguise, revealing himself to be the goddess Athina and helped Odysseus disguise himself in the tatters of a beggar, in which

Yearning for Ithaci prevails over Calypso's charms. Bottom: Odysseus brooding. Arnold Bocklin, 1883.

Top right: Nausica and her attendants discover Odysseus cast ashore on their island. John Flaxman, 1810.
Centre: Nausica. Frederick Leighton, 1879.
***Bottom:** Nausica throwing a ball. Michele Desubleo, (1602-1676).*

disguise Odysseus visited the faithful Eumeus who, though he did not recognize him, treated him courteously and put him in the picture about the true state of things on the island.

After a while **Telemachus** arrived on the isle from Sparta and went straight to Eumaeus's hut where he met his father who, casting off his disguise, revealed who he was and the two were joyfully reunited. Almost immediately they began to make plans to destroy the suitors, young noblemen who, taking advantage of Odysseus's absence had wined and dined at his expense, draining his resources dry, and laying siege to **Penelope**, forcing her to give herself to one of them in order for him to enjoy the throne of Ithaca, naturally supposing Odysseus to be dead. In order to win time, Penelope had resorted to a ruse, weaving in the morning what she unpicked at night, saying that she would only marry again when the fabric was finished.

Once more dressed as a beggar, Odysseus went to the palace. When his ancient dog, **Argos**, saw him, he wagged his tail joyfully and then gave up the ghost. Somehow the hero managed to get close enough to Penelope to tell her that her husband was still alived and, relieved and moved, she ordered her servants to look after him. One of them, an old lady, **Euriclea**, who had raised him as a boy, recognized him from a scar on his leg, but the hero made a gesture to silence her.

The following day, Penelope, who had somehow got wind of the plot, announced that she would marry whichever of the suitors could

Top right: Penelope and the suitors. John William Waterhouse. Centre: Argos, the faithful hound, recognizes Odysseus. Bottom right: Odysseus and Telemachus. Henri Lucien Doucet, 1856 – 1895.

bend Odysseus's bow and fire an arrow through twelve axe-rings; the axes to be set in a straight row, a feat that only her husband could accomplish.

In the meantime faithful shepherds and servants had been let into the secret and had managed to get old of the suitors' weapons to sequester them away.

The **suitors** tried, one by one, to bend the bow, but none of them managed. Then Odysseus asked permission to try and they all sneered at the gaunt beggar. Intervening, Telemacus said that I was only right and proper that a stranger should be given this chance.

So Odysseus bent the bow and, after he had fired an arrow through the twelve rings , turned his target on the suitors, Telemacus joining with him in taking vengeance, as well as the faithful retainers, who shut the doors to stop the suitors from escaping, until only two of them, a herald and a bard, were left, and these Odysseus spared.

At last he was reunited with Penelope, who found him much changed after so many years of suffering and hardship. Embracing him, she reassured him that she had stayed faithful to him through all the years, always trusting that he would return. Her name thus became the watchword for **marital constancy**.

After that he went and found his father, **Laertes**, who, unable to bear the excesses of the suitors, had

Top right: Evricleia, washing Odysseus's feet. 5th C. B.C.

left the palace and gone to live with the shepherds. Another joyful reunification followed.

Odysseus re-assumed his throne, restored order, made sacrifices to the gods, above all to his constant protectress, Athina, and cleansed the palace of the blood of the suitors.

After he had rested a while in peace, he remembered that when he had met Tiresias in Hades he had advised him to propitiate **Poseidon**. Shouldering an oar, he set out for new adventures, his restless, inquisitive nature not allowing him to sty for long in one place.

Passing through many lands, seeing many new sights and people, he finally arrived at a place where the people thought that his oar was some kind of farm tool and there it was he made his sacrifice to Poseidon. He returned to Ithaca but was always restless, setting out on other journeys and returning. For him it was getting to Ithaca that had value, not being there.

The end of the hero, in his deep old age, came, as Tiresias had predicted, "from the sea" when Telegonos, his son by Circe, arrived at Ithaca in search of his father and, not knowing that he was there, slaughtered some animals. When Odysseus, together with his men, came running to deal with what they thought was a raid, **Telegonos** killed his father, not knowing who he was, piercing him with a spear which had at its stip the poisonous sting of a ray. So the anger of Poseidon was vented on the much-suffering hero right to the end.

Center: Odysseus and Evrikleia. Left: Odysseus shoots the suitors. Gustav Schwab, 1882.

The poet Constantine Cavafi (1863-1933) wrote one of his most famous poems on this theme:

ITHACA

When you set out on the road to Ithaca ,
pray that the road be long,
full of adventures, full of knowledge.
The Laestrygonians and the Cyclopes,
the raging Poseidon, do not fear:
you'll never encounter suchlike on your way,
if your thoughts are raised, if fine emotion
touches your spirit and your body.
The Laestrygonians and the Cyclopes,
the fierce Poseidon you'll not encounter,
unless you carry them along within your soul,
unless your soul raises them before you.

Pray that the road be long;
that there be many a summer morning,
when with what delight, what joy,
you'll enter into harbours yet unseen;
that you may stop at Phoenician emporia
and acquire all the fine wares,
mother-of-pearl and coral, amber and ebony,
and sensuous perfumes of every kind,
as many sensuous perfumes as you can;
that you may visit many an Egyptian city,
to learn and learn again from lettered men.

Always keep Ithaca in your mind.
To arrive there is your final destination.
But do not rush the voyage at all.
Better it last for many years;
and once you're old, cast anchor on the isle,
rich with all you've gained along the way,
expecting not that Ithaca will give you wealth.

Ithaca gave you the wondrous voyage:
without her you'd never have set out.
But she has nothing to give you any more.

If then you find her poor, Ithaca has not deceived you.
As wise as you've become, with such experience, by now
you will have come to know what Ithacas really mean.

TEXT: VICKY DICKOU-ADOUERA
LAYOUT: GIORGOS PADERMOS
ART DIRECTION: MARIA KALOGRIDI
TRANSLATION INTO ENGLISH: CLIFF COOK
PRINTING:VOULGARIDIS